My Life

Robert Baldwin

My Life

from
Cotton Patches on the South Plains of Texas
to
Negotiation Tables in China and North Korea

Paperback Version

Edition 1

ISBN-13: 978-0692381748

ISBN-10: 0692381740

Author: Robert Howard Baldwin
Contributor: Mary Jane "Janie" Hamblin Boyd Baldwin
Editor: Roy D. Hickman

http://jbpress.net

to Kristi

Contents

Introduction

Part One: *Shirley*

Part Two: *Growing Up*

Part Three: *Post 2004*

Epilogue

Introduction

I had found and settled into a seat in The Dallas Cowboys Stadium. It was a little after eleven in the morning on Saturday, December 22, 2012. Earlier, when I walked into the stadium, I purchased a program. Not that I really wanted it, but it would give me something to do before the noon-time kickoff of a state championship high school football game.

Comfortable in my seat, I started thumbing through the program. I came to a sudden stop on page nine. There was a photograph which featured my late wife, Shirley. It was taken in 1955 during the state championship basketball game when Shirley's team (the Dimmitt Bobbies) defeated Granbury. In the image Shirley was about a foot off the floor with the basketball in both hands above her head. It looked as if she had just gotten a rebound.

My grandchildren's reaction to Shirley's picture was interesting. Cale was eleven and Addie nine at the time of their grandmother's death in 2004. They had known Shirley only as an older woman who was ill. Even our daughter, Kristi, did not have memories of her mother as a healthy person. In this account I want to capture the essence of the young Shirley and also share the recollections of the interesting life we had together.

It has been said a person's existence on earth has two endings—the first at death and the second when the last memory of the person disappears. A desire to have an extended mortality is also a reason why this book exists.

I am an ordinary person who had some uncommon life experiences. The word *ordinary* is open to interpretation. I use the word to indicate a person not having unique talents or exceptional mental and physical attributes. However, I have had more than my share of being in the right place at the right time. After my early years, there was an abundance of opportunities. A college education was relatively inexpensive[1] and could be obtained without outside financial assistance. The economy was good and jobs plentiful. Upward mobility within major corporations was common for those with college degrees.

The first six years after undergraduate study, I was a high school teacher. I then moved to the private sector and became a telephone man. My telephone experience began in the Bell System, and later I was an employee for the telecommunication agency of the United Nations based in Geneva, Switzerland. The UN position exposed me to locations, people, and events totally unimaginable back in my cotton boll-pulling youth. This is not to imply my life was without struggles. No life is. This book relates my encounters with difficult decisions, doubts, disease, deaths, and divorce. A spiritual story is also entwined: believer in childhood, agnostic in my forties who regained faith some twenty years later.

My life of three-quarters of a century has presented questions. Where to start? How much detail? Who is apt to be the reader? The most difficult decision has been choosing what to include as well as exclude. My memories are not a well-ordered set of events; rather, they are a hodge-podge of numerous, disjointed anecdotes.

I have tried to tell my history in a manner to give you, the reader, an understanding of who I was and to do so in an interesting format. You are the judge if I have succeeded.

Robert Baldwin
Kerrville, Texas
May 2015

---

[1] I kept a record of all expenses during my two semesters of the second year, and the total was less than $1000.

Shirley with ball in 1955 state championship game

Part One
Shirley

Chapter 1

Death

"How many more tomorrows do I have?"

My wife, Shirley, asked this question in a no-nonsense tone consistent with her personality. She was not seeking pity or even comfort. She just wanted honest information. There would be time for comfort after she had a firm grip on the truth. Shirley never wanted or allowed pity, and especially just mere hours before her death.

"Not many."

I replied with composure which might have seemed strange considering the gravity of the situation and my emotional state. To understand Shirley's purpose and my calmness, you need to comprehend the bond of trust created in the previous forty-nine years: three years of courtship and forty-six years of marriage. Those years of maturing together were not always easy, and the path to understanding was not linear. Do not interpret this to imply our marriage was unstable. Quite the contrary, it was good. Marriage, as life, is a journey, not a destination. We experienced our forty-nine-year expedition (bumps and all) in real time, and it was fun.

Shirley was a smart, strong-willed person, and I have some of these same characteristics. But by the time Shirley began to lose her independence, we were a solid team. There were no secrets concerning her medical issues. Not because she demanded, but because she was contented with reality. She did not feel sorry for herself and was a pleasure to be with during both good and bad times. I was at ease and comfortable being Shirley's spouse. Oh, how I miss her. Shirley's question opened a door of opportunity for a blessed sharing time. I thank God for it and hope my words capture the essence of that cherished night.

Shirley lay calmly in the hospice-provided bed in the master bedroom of our dream home. I was seated in a chair caressing her hand and arm. Hospice personnel had guaranteed a pain-free ending, and she assured me they had been true to their word. It was perhaps the first time she had been pain-free in years. I say perhaps because Shirley was not one to complain.

She replied in the affirmative when asked if she wanted to talk. I told her of the doctor's indication that the end would come in less than two weeks. Much affection and many tears filled our bedroom as we talked at length of our love and life together. "I have had a good life," Shirley said at some point during those precious moments. The statement was very meaningful and now provides great comfort. She also expressed a desire for a quick end. God granted her request, since as it turned out, she did not have even one more complete tomorrow. Death came the next day on July 12, 2004, just four days after our forty-sixth anniversary.

Shirley and I had never talked about or made plans for funerals. So that evening, after the tears and tenderness, I asked if she was up to giving some directives. She had only one—to be cremated. This I already knew. Being buried was not an option. Shirley was claustrophobic. My next question was regarding the dispensation of her ashes. "Just throw them beside the road somewhere," she quipped. Shirley had a dry sense of humor and a nimble wit. Becoming reflective, she revealed it was not something to which she had given much thought. I had a few ideas and asked if she wanted to hear them. She said, "Yes." My first suggestion was to purchase space in the columbarium on Highway 16 just out of Kerrville toward

Fredericksburg. "No, I don't think so," she replied. For her, that idea seemed ostentatious and a waste of money. I then asked, "Do you want me to take your ashes back to the Panhandle? There they could be spread on the farm where you lived, or be placed in the cemetery north of Hereford near the gravesites of your father and mother." Those possibilities received a polite but direct, "No."

Our daughter and son-in-law, Kristi and Stephen, had a ranch on Sand Hollow Road just north of Pearsall, Texas. Shirley and I had enjoyed many fun times there. Birthday parties for our grandchildren Cale and Addie were especially memorable. By 2004 it was difficult for Shirley to go, since she was able to walk only a few steps. But go she did, and once there, she enjoyed watching even though not being able to fully participate.

"What about the kids' ranch? Kristi and I could find a peaceful spot, and at some future date the five of us (Kristi, Stephen, Cale, Addie, and I) could spread your ashes there. We would do it on a nice day about sundown." Before I could finish she said with enthusiastic approval, "I like that." I suspect her preferring the ranch was because of who would be involved. The location for her ashes being settled, I turned our conversation to her memorial service.

"Robert, please don't overdo it."

There was a time when Shirley's request would have been totally misunderstood. Because as newlyweds our interpretation of the word *overdo* would not have been in sync. Only with time did we develop the subtlety of effective communications to avoid unmet expectations and hurt feelings. Let me try to explain.

I wrote near the beginning of this chapter that Shirley and I had some common traits. But there were also differences. Shirley was quiet and reserved, while I was loud and outgoing. I enjoyed being the center-of-attention, and she viewed seeking attention as uncouth. She was elegant and neat. To call me untidy would have been kind. I was more tolerant of faults of others. She had high standards for herself and expected much the same in others. Neither of us was high tempered. Bouts of anger were rare, seldom intense, and never prolonged; by mid-marriage, they were almost extinct. We had diverging approaches when upset. Shirley would voice disapproval immediately. I was not apt to verbalize my displeasures. The proverbial fly-on-the-wall in our first apartment would have occasionally heard Shirley say phrases like: *Stop being silly, Grow-up,* or *You have the same set of clothes in which to get just as happy as you are now upset.* If that fly read my mind, the thoughts were in the nature of, *Ease up, Oh, Mrs. Perfect,* or my all-time favorite *Well, Missy, sometimes life is just not fair.* Thankfully, that young couple of the late nineteen fifties had successfully learned to accommodate and even appreciate our differences. I understood well what Shirley meant when she said, "Robert, please don't overdo it." Her cautionary request was like the rote *be careful* statement a parent makes to a responsible, adult child.

Kristi and I had recently completed plans for Shirley's memorial service. It was gratifying to share our ideas and outline the tentative schedule with Shirley. She was pleased. I had arranged for close friends to send their memories and had already received a couple of the tributes and a few condolences via e-mail. It would take time to print them; and the wisdom of leaving her, even briefly, during those irreplaceable moments was not a given.

"Do you want me to print out some of these and read them to you?"

"Please."

I cannot recall exactly which were read. But my memory of Shirley's serene delight is vivid. She said very little. Her few verbal responses were things such as *How kind of her* and *We did have fun.* Her friends' humorous quips brought relaxed smiles. After reading about a half-dozen items, Shirley whispered she was very tired. It had been a long, emotionally draining evening; but oh, so enriching. "You get some rest, and I will read more tomorrow," were the last words I know for sure Shirley heard. She quickly fell into a tranquil sleep, so quiet I had to get very near to know she was still breathing.

Our master bedroom is spacious, but in order to place Shirley's hospital bed near the bathroom, our bed frame had been removed. The box springs and mattress were placed on the floor providing a place for me to rest and sleep. Sometime during that night, Shirley said, "Robert, my feet are cold." I got up and put additional cover over her feet and gently rubbed them through the covers. "Is that better?" My question received no response as she was again quietly sleeping.

Waking the next morning, I found Shirley asleep in the same position. I heard no sound or saw no movement that final day. I was present when she took her last breath but was not able to detect it. Her death was sometime in the late afternoon. The Certificate of Death has the time of death at six in the afternoon and immediate cause as Endstage Renal Disease.

***

Kristi and I decided on the man-made pond at the ranch for spreading Shirley's ashes. A few weeks after her death, on a nice day about sundown, the five of us rode from the house to the pond. We climbed on the boulders at the edge of the pond. From there we took turns spreading Shirley's ashes atop the placid water. I spread the largest and last portion. Some sank upon hitting the water, and others drifted slowly toward the western sunset.

If Stephen and Kristi still own the ranch at my death, I want most of my ashes to be with Shirley's. But I want a small portion placed in the Guadalupe River near the large cypress tree where Cale and Addie would catch minnows in their just-emptied ICEE cups.

While heading back to the house, Stephen asked if there was anything I wanted him to do for me. "Yes, take me back to the Friday night in the summer of 1955 when I walked into Streun's barn and saw Shirley for the first time."

Pond where Shirley's ashes were spread

Chapter 2

Streun's Barn

In the summer of 1955 George and Annie DeLozier lived on their farm located about fourteen miles from Dimmitt near the western boundary of Castro County. The area was sparsely populated. Granted, there were more people than a few generations earlier when ranching still defined the economics. Single-family farms like the DeLozier's had become the main way to make a living early in the twentieth century in this area of Texas. Families lived on the same flat land where their crops were grown. Milo, wheat, and corn were the staples, with perhaps a little cotton. Some braved the market volatility of truck-farm products such as potatoes, onions, and carrots, but not George. To have an allotment for sugar beets was like money in the bank. George had no sugar-beet allotment and only a marginal amount of money in the bank.

A quarter of a section (one hundred and sixty acres) was about the minimum needed to provide for a family of four. George and Annie owned ten acres more than a *labor*[2] which is about 177 acres. The land ownership patterns were mostly square or rectangular tracts with sides in a north-to-south and east-to-west alignment. The roads owned and maintained by Castro County had the same orientation. These county roads divided the land into plots, the sizes of which were a

---

[2] There are a number of Spanish units of measurement of length and area now obsolete. They include the *vara, league,* and *labor.* The *vara* a unit of length of thirty-three and one third inches in Texas (it is thirty-three inches in California). *League* and *labor* are units used to express the areas of land. A *league* equal to 25 million square *varas* and is equivalent to about 4,428.4 acres. A *labor* equals 1 million square *varas,* or about 177 acres.

mixture of *Sections* (an English land unit of six hundred and forty acres) and *Leagues*. The DeLozier's land was in the northwest part of Capital Lands League 490. That league was part of the XIT Ranch. The XIT Ranch in the 1880's was the largest range in the world under fence. It was created from acreage awarded to Abner Taylor and the Farwell brothers of Chicago by the state of Texas in exchange for construction of the pink granite state capitol building in Austin.

The farm families had neighbors, but they were not close. A quarter of a mile was about the shortest distance between houses, with a half mile or greater being more common. One need only step outside and look for trees to locate a neighbor's home site. There were almost no trees other than those planted near the scattered houses. Generally the trees were mature English elms. Most of the houses were not large, with whitewashed stucco exteriors, an upgrade covering the original wood siding. A few new larger dwellings with brick facades were in the area, but I do not recall any being near the DeLozier's place.

In addition to a five-room house with no indoor bath; George and Annie had a dilapidated one-car garage, granary, chicken house, cow shed with pen, pig pen, a windmill with a raised water storage tank, and a root cellar. George and Annie had four children: Wayne, Willis, Shirley, and Lee. By the summer of 1955, only Shirley and Lee were still living at home. They would be returning to Dimmitt High School in the fall, Shirley as a senior and Lee a sophomore. Wayne was in Lubbock and working in the cotton business. Willis had graduated from Texas Tech and been drafted into the Army. He was stationed in an eastern state doing military work sensitive enough he could not talk about it. I don't think it rose to the level of his saying, "If I tell you, I will have to kill you." Shirley was proud of him, and the secrecy of his position impressed me. As the only daughter, Shirley was given deference not just by George and Annie but also from her brothers who called her *Sis*. After Shirley and I became a couple, the benefits of her position in the family also accrued to me—especially from Annie.

Living near the edge of the Dimmitt school district's northwest boundary allowed George to supplement the farm income by driving a school bus. It was a win-win situation for the school district and George but not so great for Shirley and Lee. During the school year George's bus was parked overnight at the farm. Thus, Shirley and Lee were the first on and the last off the bus. George worked at Hays Implement in Dimmitt during school hours. While the rest of the family was in Dimmitt, Annie kept the house, cared for the vegetable garden, and drove the tractor tilling the land. By late May or early June of 1955, George had returned the bus to the school district's barn. He had transitioned back to full-time farming, not realizing decisions and actions occurring one hundred and thirty miles to the south were soon to impact his family.

***

Howard and Blanche Baldwin were in the process of relocating their family from the sandy farm country around Wellman to Frio, Texas, a community six miles south of Hereford. My new home was thirteen and three-tenths miles from the DeLozier's farm, mostly north but a little east. I, like George, had no clue how important this move would be in the lives of his daughter and me. It is frightening now when I remember how much I did not want to make the move. Transferring to a different school was not an issue because I had done that four times (five if I count the Lubbock school attended in the summer term between the third and fourth grades). But this adjustment was just prior to my senior year. Basketball was more than a passion; it was my life. There was no hardship clause in the eligibility rules then. Therefore, changing schools meant I would not be allowed to play. I tried to convince Daddy to let me stay with the family of a friend in Wellman, if not the entire school year, at least until the end of the basketball season. When George first met me, he may have wished I had been successful in persuading my father.

There is something very interesting about the dynamics between a father, his daughter, and that hairy-legged guy who has caught her eye. A father's protective response is very understandable. Having been a suitor, a dad, and now a grandfather of an adolescent girl, I view a father's reaction as something more subtle and deeper. Of course he wants to shield her from hurt and harm. There is also a desire to hold on to a moment in time. It is not that he doesn't want his daughter to mature and build a life of her own. But why, oh why, must it happen so fast?

Whatever early misgivings George may have harbored about Shirley's interest in me dissipated in time, if not soon after our marriage, but for sure after the birth of his granddaughter, Kristi.

My father and mother just might have had a touch of divine intervention concerning this relocation. I think so.

The communities contained within the Hereford-Dimmitt-Friona triangle did not have exact boundaries. To this day, it is not clear to me where the communities of Frio and Easter stop and start, but it seemed to be obvious to the natives. Each of these two communities had only a single landmark—I'm not sure if there were more in the past. For Easter, it was a small corrugated-tin grain elevator; for Frio, an old red-brick building which was originally built for the community school.

The old school building was then the meeting location for the Frio Baptist Church. The church had recently called the Rev. Howard Baldwin as their pastor. Along with Howard the church obtained another valuable asset—his wife Blanche. They also welcomed three boys: my two younger brothers (Godfrey and Eugene) and me. My two older sisters Mary and Wynelle already were married, and Olagene and Darold were students at West Texas State. The church owned a parsonage about a half-mile north of the red-brick building. That house was our home.

West of Frio was the small town of Summerfield. It had a post office with a small store, a dozen or so houses, and a Baptist church. The DeLozier farm was a few miles south of the town. But when asked, Shirley would say she was from Summerfield. She and her family were members and regular attendees of the Summerfield Baptist Church.

High school aged members in the Frio and Summerfield congregations were about equal in number, twelve to fifteen. Most attended Hereford High School, and those who did not went to Dimmitt. Social dividing lines (school and church) were nebulous between the two groups. The atmosphere was relaxed and pleasurable whenever the two groups came together. Friday nights and Sunday afternoons were when they joined for fun and games, and these good times would happen three or four time during summer *vacations*. I put vacations in italics because farm work made me look forward to the fall and the start of school—even football two-a-day practices did not seem so bad.

The first Sunday I attended the Frio church, Clark Dobbs, a member near my age, cautioned me to be careful when talking about others since most everyone was related to the Andrews or Sparkmans—for some, both. It became true for me later when Godfrey married

Delores Andrews and Bonnie Sparkman became Eugene's bride.

Very soon after my arrival in Frio, a Friday night volleyball match between the team from Frio versus the team from Summerfield was scheduled to be played in Streun's barn. I didn't know where Summerfield was and could not have spelled the name Streun even if given the first four letters. But it sounded like fun and a great opportunity to get some new-kid-in-town attention. I went with a car load which included Don Mobley and Clark Dobbs. I don't remember who else was in the car.

Annie DeLozier's sister, Allie Faye, was married to Jack Streun, and they farmed and had cattle on a place which backed up to the dry (except after heavy rains) Frio draw. Their land was about five miles north of the DeLozier's place. Jack Streun was one of the few men whom I would call a real cowboy. Jack and Allie Faye had two sons, Joe and Gene. Joe was tall and had played college basketball for West Texas State. Gene was Shirley's and my age. I did not know him in the summer of 1955. But that fall, we became classmates and friends. The Streuns had a large Quonset hut-style barn which worked great for lighted night volleyball games.

We were one of the last car loads to arrive. The barn had large sliding doors at each end allowing entry and exit for large farm equipment. We entered thru the east door. I followed Don, Clark and the others in.

There she was!

Standing with a small group from Summerfield, half profile and half facing the door I had entered.

There she was!

Standing tall and erect in a confident but not cocky manner.

There she was!

Wearing neat, just pressed jeans, and a cotton buttoned-down-the-front blouse with the shirttail out.

<u>There she was!</u>

Looking so very attractive.

Some images become permanently etched in the brain, and Shirley's image that night is one of mine.

She turned her head slightly and glanced as I entered. I know she saw me, but there was no indication of interest on her part. Shirley and her immediate family were people whose emotions did not deviate much—neither positive nor negative—from a stable flat line.

No one introduced us, and I was not bold enough to approach her. During the teenage chatter before play began, we made brief eye contact a couple of times, and she had a gentle, soft expression in response to my smile. I took that as positive, but any response less than her coming over and slapping me would not have dampened my desire to know her.

It was obvious from the beginning of the game she was the most skilled volleyball player in the barn. It was my planning, not just good luck, which brought us face-to-face the first time I rotated from the backcourt to the net. There we made steady eye contact. I leaned in close to the net, and she did also, sensing I wanted to say something only she would hear. In a low voice I said, "Your net play has been making some of my teammates look pretty bad, and I think it's only fair to let you know now I am at net, things will be different." She just smiled. Soon thereafter she hit a spike which I tried to block, but the ball went through my hands and hit my head. "Just luck," I whispered to her. She said nothing but smiled with a twinkle in her eye.

I left Streun's barn without any further interaction with her and not even knowing her name. But it had been a good night, and playing basketball for the Wellman Wildcats my senior year seemed much less significant. Funny how quickly a girl can change the priorities of an adolescent boy.

On the ride back to Frio I asked Don, "Who was the tall, good looking girl from Summerfield?"

"I noticed you eying her. That's Shirley DeLozier, a classmate at Dimmitt. She is quiet, very nice, and a heck of a basketball player." The image in my brain now had a name attached.

Streun's Barn (picture taken in 2013)

Shirley in 1955

Chapter 3

First Date

Making money during the summer months was a necessity. In 1955 I drove a tractor for Frank Robbins, a member of the Frio church. After the volleyball game in Streun's barn, I had a greater objective than the mundane pursuit of adding to my meager bank account. Learning more about a girl named Shirley DeLozier was high on my summer to-do list. I had moderate success with the money thing but didn't do so well with the learning part. Before providing additional details regarding my efforts to get Shirley's attention, perhaps a little background concerning girls and me in general would be helpful.

Except for a major crush on Essie Moore in the third grade, I had never had a girlfriend. It was not for lack of interest. Wellman High School had less than seventy students, and my class had only fifteen. There were a few couples going steady, with the rest of us hanging out as a group. On Saturday nights we guys would go to Brownfield, take in a movie and check out the girls. Not just the ones from Wellman but also the girls from Union, Meadow, and Ropes. But not the girls from Brownfield; we small-town boys seemed to be intimidated by city girls. After the movie, it was out to Boston's Super Dog for a coke and then to go drag the square around the Terry County Court House. We would holler at the cars full of girls and at times stop beside one and flirt through the rolled down windows. This ritual was less risky than the possibility of rejection if I asked a girl for a real date. In fact, I had only one real date before the summer of 1955.

To be a real date, the boy must ask the girl to go exclusively with him to a movie, have a coke, and drag the Square with no attention given to anyone else. Thus, school functions such as the annual FFA Chicken Barbecue did not count, since most boys drove a girl there, but once in the cafeteria it was a group thing. For me, double dating with my older brother Darold also did not count, since I was to be the driver, and most of the time his girlfriend would set-up my date. No chance of my ego being damaged by a rebuff with that arrangement.

Sometime during my junior year, I summoned the courage to ask Danny Loe. She said, "Yes." Her being a freshman may have increased my chances of acceptance. This was not the reason I chose her. She was very nice and someone whose company would be a pleasure. Except for the awkward conversation with Mr. Loe prior to Danny and me leaving, my memory is of an enjoyable evening. I'm not sure why I never asked her out again.

My limited experience did not provide an adequate guide of how to approach Shirley. However, I knew she was special, and I did not want to make a clumsy mistake.

Shirley and I were never formally introduced, but that was not uncommon among the youth of Frio and Summerfield. Most everyone knew all the others and had for a long time. New teenagers became known and got to know others by osmosis. Just be there and join in, and soon you were accepted. We were in a common group only a couple of times after the first volleyball game. We never talked directly to each other. By paying attention and asking stealthy questions, I was able to guess she did not have a steady boyfriend. But I was not sure since Charles Jacks had brought her to Streun's barn the night of our first meeting. I was completely oblivious to that fact at the time. Being an optimist, it helped explain Shirley's muted response to my flirtation.

By summer's end I would have answered "Yes" if asked if I knew Shirley DeLozier, meaning I had only a name linked to her face. In reality I knew nothing compared to what I wanted to know. What made her happy and sad? What were her passions and interests? Was she smart and kind? Did she have a sense of humor, and most important of all—had she noticed me and if so, did she want to learn and understand who I was?

An opportunity arose unexpectedly soon after the beginning of the school year. The occasion was the first football game between Dimmitt and Silverton. It was a little strange as I would not be playing. In a small school like Wellman, not playing football was the exception. However, the larger student population at Hereford made a real difference. There were about 400 students in high school, with just over 100 in my senior class. Thus, not playing football was common. Of the few boys I knew, none played. As different as it was for me, it was even more so for Daddy. At Wellman he was high school principal and had coached football. He had always been totally immersed with football there. His first position in Hereford was as a sixth grade mathematics teacher. He knew few if any players on the high school team. Don Mobley was the quarterback for Dimmitt, and his being a member of the Frio church gave Daddy the incentive to attend Dimmitt's game. Of course I liked Daddy's game selection because Shirley was apt to be there. He didn't yet know about her!

As was Daddy's habit, he and I arrived at the Dimmitt stadium early. While Daddy was greeting and meeting people near the bottom of the steps leading up to the home-team stands, I was scouting for the most strategic seat. (A side note: there were two types of people in Daddy's world—the ones he knew and the ones he soon would know). I found the perfect location— about half-way up, near but not in the Dimmitt student section and isolated from other fans. When Shirley arrived and headed toward her friends, she would not be able to miss seeing me seated alone.

I saw Shirley walking toward the stands. Coming up the steps she scanned the bleachers and spotted me. Without hesitation, she came to sit beside me and said, "I was hoping you would be here."

Her actions and words lowered my anxiety level. Our dialogue was light but not full of adolescent giddiness. While relatively quiet in a crowd, Shirley was a good conversationalist in one-on-one situations. Family, friends, school, church, likes, and dislikes were some of the various items we discussed. The chat was open and free flowing. There was limited focus on the football game. For the record Dimmitt won the game eighteen to zero. Asking her if she would join me for a movie the next night was easy, and I was not surprised at her acceptance. That Friday night in bleachers filled with boisterous football fans, two people who had just met were able to create a space for only themselves. Our ability to do this would prove to be a valuable asset. We said our good-byes in the stands after the game.

As Daddy and I were walking to the car, I had feelings never experienced before. I was physically attracted to Shirley at first sight in Streun's barn. After talking with her under those Friday night lights, I also found her emotionally and intellectually irresistible. My hope and prayer as I mentally replayed that evening's events before falling asleep was that Shirley had similar feelings.

Daddy and I talked about the game and Don's quarterbacking. Don had played well. Changing the subject, Daddy said, "Son, I had a strange experience tonight. I was talking to some people when this good-looking girl walked by. When one of her parents asked her where she was going, her reply was 'I am going up and sit with Robert'. I thought, 'Is she talking about my

24

Robert?' So I watched where she went, and it was you. Who is she?"

"Her name is Shirley DeLozier, and she goes to the Summerfield church. I met her playing volleyball this summer, and may I use the car tomorrow night because she and I want to take in a movie?"

***

Shirley had given me directions to her house at the football game, but I had not yet mastered the local landmarks. Therefore, finding her house that Saturday evening was a little difficult. However, I managed to get Daddy's two-tone red and white DeSoto to her house near the appointed time of our first date. There were some awkward moments before Shirley and I left her house. The front door on which I knocked was seldom used by family or friends. Lee answered and we introduced ourselves. Shirley had talked to me about him the night before. I sat on the living-room sofa and Lee in a chair while we made polite but stilted conversation. George and Annie came in briefly for an introduction. I did not ask, and Lee did not say why Shirley had not made an appearance. Lee was doing his best to entertain me, but after a few minutes he excused himself. I am sure the time alone was much shorter than it seemed. Shirley finally came in. She made sure I had met all the family. We left with Annie saying, "Have fun and don't be out too late."

Carmen Jones starring Dorothy Dandridge and Harry Belafonte was the movie playing at the Carlile Theater in Dimmitt. We had to sit close to the screen due to a large crowd. After the movie, we went to the drive-in hamburger place frequented by the high school students. I believe it was called the Bobcat Den. We had cokes and a bite to eat and then drove around Dimmitt with Shirley telling me who was in the other cars.

I drove slowly as we talked while returning to her house. It was fun, and I had her back home at an early hour. I walked her to the back door, and we said our good byes, but not before she had agreed to go out with me the next Saturday. No good night kiss or even holding hands—that would come in due time.

Shirley & me (1956)

Chapter 4

Courtship

I was on an emotional high, but that was soon to change. A person who can make your spirits soar is also able to snap you back into reality in a blink-of-the-eye. Prior to the summer of 1955 Shirley had not been waiting for me to appear so she could start her life.

Elvis Presley was the star attraction of a concert at the City Auditorium in Amarillo on Thursday, October 13. Our first date was on September 10 about a month prior to this big event. Before our next scheduled movie outing of September 17, I did a careful review of my financial situation. Ordinarily the high costs of a top-talent concert would have prevented my going. Did I say Johnny Cash was also to perform? Shirley was special and it was Elvis, so I would somehow fit it into my budget.

The anticipation of her joy when informed of my plans made waiting until Saturday difficult. We had barely left her house when I told her the good news. Her response momentarily stunned me and then left my thinking in a state of disarray for a few days.

Shirley was in fact going to see Elvis with Don Glenn. Don was four or five years her senior. He had already finished school and had a good paying job.

Shirley then revealed the reason for her delayed entry into the living room the week before. Soon after I had entered her house via the front door, Don had knocked on the back door. It may seem strange someone would just show up without an appointment. But the DeLoziers had no telephone, and in the rural setting of the nineteen fifties, it was not uncommon.

I do not know the content of the discussions in the back of the house the night of our first date, but I do know the outcome. Shirley would go to the movie with me, but she would not break her commitment to Don concerning the Elvis concert.

While Shirley and I were on a date soon after October 13, I asked her, "How was the concert?"

"Ok."

I do not remember it ever being mentioned again.

***

We both settled into our final year of high school. My transition into Hereford High School was not difficult. There were Hereford girls who would have been interesting to me if I had not already met Shirley. Honestly, I did not desire to date others.

The roads between the Frio parsonage and her house became very familiar to me. During the rest of football season we saw each other three or four additional times. The frequency dropped during basketball season due to her playing for the Dimmitt Bobbies while I was doing game statistics in some different gymnasium for the Hereford Whitefaces. However, it did not hamper our growing closer. Each time we were together my comfort level increased. It seemed as if each had known the other for years instead of weeks. I do not remember it being specifically expressed, but by the end of basketball season our relationship had become exclusive.

The mighty Dimmitt Bobbies were feared and well known, not just in the South Plains and Panhandle area but also in the entire state. They had won the state championship the two previous years, and Shirley was one of their better players. For her senior season Dimmitt had been placed into a new district which included Tulia, another strong team. They tied for the district championship, each with one loss. Then only the champion advanced to the playoffs. Tulia won the coin toss so the tie-breaking game was played in the Tulia gymnasium. I rode with George, Annie and Lee to Tulia. Shirley went on the bus with her team members. Dimmitt lost seventy-eight to seventy-six in a game well played by both teams. Shirley performed very well, scoring thirty-six points. She rode back to Dimmitt with her family and me.

I was more disappointed than Shirley at not getting to go to the state tournament in Austin. Once the white, high top Converse All Stars shoes were laced up, and the game's opening jump ball tossed, no one had more focus, hustle, and intensity than Shirley—no one! However, after a game was over, she would not let a loss ruin her day. Both of these traits were just who Shirley was. I saw some similar behaviors in our granddaughter, Addie Williams, in the fall of 2012, when the Pearsall varsity volleyball team lost an exciting final match of Addie's senior season. Most of Addie's senior friends were not taking the defeat well. Addie had played well and hard, and she was ready to move on.

***

Courtship is a time of discovery, not just for the two people directly involved, but also for their families. Shirley and I had begun to attend family functions of each other. Annie and I hit it off well from the beginning. Lee and I also became friends. It was a little different with George. It was not bad, just not a relaxed situation. Time works wonders, and while we never became best buddies, we did develop a mutual love and respect. Daddy and Shirley's relationship mirrored mine and Annie's, and Shirley related to Mother in somewhat the same fashion as I did with George. I don't think Shirley and Mother ever obtained the same level of understanding as George and I, but they made their relationship work.

Each family had a slightly different dynamic. A large group of DeLoziers was subdued compared to the more boisterous Baldwin family gatherings. Many of the DeLozier family members had *green thumbs*, thus there was always some talk of the condition of their various flowers, vegetable gardens, and inside plants. Shirley had success with both her flower beds and house plants everywhere we lived. Talking about church and school issues was more common for the Baldwins.

Shirley and I had similar history concerning birth and early childhood which may have helped in our assimilation into each other's family. George and Annie had married in Texas where their first child, Wayne, was born. From Texas they moved to Sevier County in Tennessee, the birth place for their other three children. Shirley's date of birth was November 1, 1937.

My parents relocated from Texas to New Mexico prior to my birth on August 23, 1938. I was born in the ranch house of my Baldwin grandparents near Pie Town, New Mexico. Both families moved back to Texas in 1942 (an interesting coincidence). Thus, childhood trips back to the places of our births were normal. At Baldwin family gatherings there was always reminiscing about the New Mexico years, and the DeLoziers did the same for their time in Tennessee.

The DeLoziers' harking back seemed natural even though I had never been to east Tennessee, and their stories created a desire to see the hills and hollers and to meet Shirley's relatives still living there. Therefore, it is not surprising our first major trip after marriage was to Shirley's place of birth. I desired to go, and my ego believes Shirley was pleased for her kinfolks to meet me.

***

Fall of 1956 found me and other incoming freshmen standing on the grass at the rear of the main administration building at Texas Technological College in Lubbock. Orientation information was blaring from the outdoor speakers. Shirley was there with me. It was an exciting time for me, but not so much for Shirley.

We had known each other for more than a year, and spent lots of time together. When talking with others, Shirley was always genuine, be it a casual acquaintance or best friend. However, she kept a tight guard on who would have access to her most intimate thoughts and feelings. Our relationship had progressed to knowing each other well. Shirley did not have aspirations to obtain a college degree. She had the ability and study ethic, but her priorities did not include a formal education after high school. George and his daughter were at odds about this, and I had good enough judgment to not get involved. The issue was resolved by Shirley agreeing to give college a try for one semester. If it did not work for her, then she could find a job. I was happy she would be on campus with me for at least the first semester of my freshman year.

Delores Battles, a classmate from Dimmitt, roomed with Shirley in Knapp Hall. I was in West Hall with two roommates, Norman Bookout and Robert "Willy" Williams in a room designed for just two people. Dorm space was tight that fall. Willy was from Pearland, a town near Houston. We had not known each other until arriving on campus. He became a good friend, and Frio being much closer to Lubbock than Pearland, he was a welcome guest at my house and also at the

DeLozier's farm. During that fall semester, Willy would accompany Shirley and me to movies, bowling, and the Bell Dairy malt shop in Lubbock. History may be repeating itself as my grandson, Cale Williams, seems to tag along on outings with his University of Texas roommate Colin and his girlfriend. The pattern was also there in the generation between Cale and me. Stephen and Kristi's dating always seemed to include Lester, a friend of Stephen. In fact the first image of Stephen seen by Shirley and me was a picture Kristi brought to Puerto Rico, and the photo was of three, not just her and Stephen.

Final grades after the first semester thinned the student population, so for the spring term I moved into a room with Don Zimmerman. Both Norman Bookout and Don were members of my Hereford senior class.

Shirley's college life was a one-and-done involvement. She did well in her studies and seemed to enjoy the campus atmosphere. However, the experience did not change her mind. So her formal education ended at the close of Tech's 1956 fall semester. Her brother Willis was on Christmas leave and moved Shirley and her belongings from Knapp Hall back with George and Annie in Summerfield. Shirley started a job search. I also had plans.

Money management was a strong suit for Shirley. I was not terrible when handling finances, but my skills were amateurish compared to hers. We both had an aversion to spending hard-earned money by paying interest charges. Thus, items were not to be purchased until there was enough cash. Other than houses and land the only item I remember our buying on-time was a chest-type freezer. It was purchased soon after our marriage. Freezing vegetables from the DeLozier's garden had to be done during the harvest season, and having a place to preserve them could not wait until money was saved.

I wanted to ask Shirley to marry me but could not do so until I had an engagement ring. Early in the spring semester of 1957, I started saving and shopping. Before the end of the school year I had put aside enough to purchase an inexpensive matching engagement ring-wedding band set.

The eighty miles or so between Lubbock and the DeLozier's farm had changed our dating habits. I had no automobile, so I would hitchhike to see Shirley. Usually Lynn Jones, the vice president of my Hereford senior class, and I would go together. I had a laundry bag with Tech's logo on it. So getting people to give us a ride was not a major issue. In fact, Lynn and I would turn down undesirable offers with the hope a better one would soon arrive. My job as a busboy at the Spur Restaurant also limited trips.

Not long after obtaining the rings, I made a trip home. During this trip I would propose to Shirley. I did not tell Mother and Daddy of my plans, so they assumed it was just another movie date when I asked to use the DeSoto.

My excitement level was off the charts while driving to her house with the velveteen box containing the engagement ring safely stored in the glove compartment. After picking Shirley up, I drove about a mile from her house and stopped the car on the dirt country road. I removed the box from the glove compartment and opened it showing her the ring. I'm not sure what I said, if anything. It was not a surprise to her. She took the ring from the box and put it on the third finger of her left hand. Holding her hand with palm facing away, she looked at the ring while turning her hand to different angles. Turning to me, we embraced in a long passionate kiss and a couple more.

"Let's go back to the house," she said.

Annie seemed pleased, and George just said, "What took so long?"

Did he mean the time it took for me to propose and Shirley to accept before returning to let them know, or was he wondering why I had not asked her months earlier? At the time I thought it was the former; now I am not so sure.

Shirley and me (1957)

Chapter 5

Engagement

We started making plans the evening I gave Shirley the engagement ring. Not concerning a wedding ceremony but agreeing on items of a higher importance. Shirley was practical, and I had the ability to listen and reason. We agreed our most immediate priority was my completion of a college education. Having a degree would be in the best interest for both our joint and individual goals.

Shirley stated again her long-term objectives were to be my wife and a stay-at-home mother of our children. It was clear to both of us to become husband and wife quickly was not wise. First, we would need some necessities: automobile, furniture, kitchen utensils, bed and bath linens, and a little money in the bank to pay bills. Shirley would find a job and start saving for the items on our needs list. I would continue school and look for a better paying job than farm work for the summer. Our desire was to get married as soon as possible within our prerequisites. Therefore, selecting an exact wedding date would have to wait.

Shirley had obtained a clerical position with Pioneer Natural Gas Company in Hereford. Renting a bedroom in the Knight Street house of her Grandmother Lance proved not to be a good idea. Thus, I picked her up for dates only a few times at that location. A small garage apartment owned by Thelma McMinn, a DeLozier family friend, became her next abode. The space and rent were shared with Sandra Glenn, a younger sister of Don. These accommodations worked well. Sandra had just finished high school in Dimmitt and was working in Hereford.

Shirley made it very clear to me she would work outside our home only until I received an undergraduate degree. I wondered if she might change her mind, but she did not. At that time, her choice was not uncommon or controversial. She never expressed any regrets to me concerning her decision.

Some of life's decisions have far greater effect on the future than anticipated at the time they are made. The reverse is also true. Reflecting back, Shirley's life desire as expressed prior to our marriage was very significant in setting the tone of our life together. Things and actions became *ours,* not *mine* and *yours.* Shirley paid me a high compliment by entrusting her economic future in my unproven abilities. I think she saw potential in me of which I was not aware. But also she did not allow failure to be an option.

I would have adjusted to her having a career more than wife and mother if that had been her selection. My guess is Shirley understood the importance of her role election from the beginning. A correct equilibrium of being an effective spouse in the oneness of a healthy marriage, and at the same time maintaining an appropriate level of individuality is not always easy and apt to be unique in subtle but meaningful actions and thoughts. The following anecdote from our retirement years may help give a feel of Shirley's and my abilities to obtain the right balance.

Curt and Connie Bergan were friends. Shirley and Connie enjoyed like interests: gourmet cooking, artistic creativeness (Connie's was quilting and Shirley's needlepoint), and home décor and maintenance. Curt and I had been secondary school teachers just out of college and then changed to private sector business. Curt was very successful, and had retired at an early age. I also had a comfortable level of success followed by early retirement. We both enjoyed golf and high school sports.

Curt's and my friendship at that time was such we shared personal and sensitive issues. One night Curt and I were returning to Kerrville from the Texas Boys High School Basketball tournament played in Austin when Curt asked me if Shirley resented the money I spent on golf.

"I don't think so. You should ask her," I replied. I then asked him to explain his interest.

"Connie and I were discussing it recently, and there seems to be a disparity. Shirley does not have a passion requiring an equivalent amount of time and resources spent by you for golf."

Curt's golf and Connie's passion for quilting seemed to offset each other.

The next time all four of us were together, Curt asked Shirley if she had a desire requiring equal time and resources.

"No."

"Do you resent Robert's golf time and expenses since you don't have something comparable?"

"No."

"Why not?" he inquired with a slight hint of amazement.

Shirley retorted matter-of-factly, "Because I know I could have something comparable, if I wanted."

***

The summer of 1957 was to be my last period of living with my parents. That summer I measured cotton acreages for the government's allotment program. Less physical effort and more pay than farm work was not a bad deal. Being a little older and out of high school had its rewards. But the job required a vehicle. I spent $200 to purchase a used 1946 Ford. Bad brakes and water pump that vapor locked two to three times per day made driving from farm-to-farm an interesting summer. I remember I was able to sell the car for $50 at summer's end.

Come fall I did not live on campus. Off-campus living and eating was less expensive. I found one of three second-floor bedrooms in the home of a widow who lived on Fifteenth Street less than three blocks from College Avenue, and I ate two meals per day in a boarding house a couple of blocks from my rented bedroom.

Soon after the start of classes, I landed a job with good pay but not so good working hours. It was for the TNM&O Bus Company. A couple of other Tech students and I washed and serviced the buses at night. We started at midnight and worked until six to eight the next morning, five days per week except during football season. During the season we worked one more night cleaning the charter buses used by the schools and fans.

My classes were scheduled mostly in the mornings. After lunch I would study until about four or five in the afternoon and then sleep for five to six hours.

Don Ed Robinson was already living in one of the other two bedrooms in the widow's house when I moved in. I did not know he was living there until signing the rental agreement. Don and I knew each other when he had been a member of the Frio Baptist Church. He finished Dimmitt High School one year after Shirley. He and I had little contact during my freshman year at Tech. He now had a job at Piggly Wiggly Supermarket Number Seven on Nineteenth Street, and was an incoming freshman at Tech that fall of fifty-seven.

There were two others facts about Don that turned out to be very fortunate for me. First, he had an automobile, and second (and even more important) he was dating Sandra Glenn, Shirley's roommate. He would be making trips to Hereford and stopping at Shirley's front door step! With me paying for the gasoline, we made as many trips as money, time, and schedules allowed.

Shirley's paycheck from the gas company and good money management skills allowed her to purchase the basic furniture needed to fill a one-bedroom apartment: a three piece living room set, a bedroom group (bed with headboard, dresser, and night stand), and a four-chair chrome dinette set. All of these new items she had in storage and ready for our use by May of 1958.

During my second year of college my grades were not good; in fact, I ended the spring semester on scholastic probation. But it was not a bad time for my bank account. By spring a wedding date somewhere near mid-summer seemed to be a financial possibility. Just a few details would need to fall into place.

Our marriage plans included Shirley arranging a transfer from the gas company's Hereford office to the one in Lubbock. This proved to be no problem. Not only did they approve the transfer, she was allowed a week of paid leave for the wedding and a brief honeymoon.

At the end of the spring semester in mid-May the bus company had agreed for me to begin work at 10 pm, thus earning eight hours of pay per night. I had also arranged for a job at a bottled water company to work two hours in the morning and another hour in the afternoon.

The bottled water company work consisted mostly of loading and unloading trucks. The water was bottled in five-gallon glass containers with screw-on metal lids.

Each full bottle weighed just over forty pounds. Placing the ones in the top row of the trucks required me to lift them above my head.

I did not attend the summer term, so with no classes or studying I was able to get six to seven hours of sleep each day.

The last name of the man in charge of the water bottling operation was Young. Mr. and Mrs. Young were in their early sixties. He and I established a good rapport, and Shirley and I subsequently became good friends with the Youngs. Mr. Young purchased a new Chevrolet each year. When I started working at the water company, he had a 1958 two-tone green and white Biscayne with about 1,500 miles. Upon learning he was planning to trade it in on a new 1959 model, I asked whether he had any interest in selling me his used one. He agreed to sell it to me for $600 which was less than the trade value. This was a kind gesture. Shirley learned later Mrs. Young had major input, and her motivation was to help a young couple get a good start in their marriage. The Youngs' new car would be arriving in late June, so Shirley and I would have an automobile near the first of July.

Sometime about the middle of June, I learned from an acquaintance about a couple who were opening a sandwich and donut shop in downtown Lubbock. They would need some help for a couple of weeks during the start-up phase. They hired me, thus I had a third paying job. I worked about an hour in the mornings running the donut-making machine and an hour or so at the noon rush. At noon I mostly waited and cleaned the few tables available for the dine-in customers.

One day the cook did not show, and the owner wanted to know if I could fill in for him. I did fine except for the lettuce and tomatoes added to a grilled cheese sandwich. Hey, I had never even heard of a grilled cheese sandwich! The customer thought it was funny and ate it saying, "It was certainly different—but not bad."

At some point Shirley and I were confident we would soon arrive at a position of being able to support ourselves as husband and wife. I'm not sure what the tipping point was—maybe it was the car arrangements—that allowed us to set our wedding date as July 8, 1958. I do not remember the exact timing of setting the date, but for sure it was far enough before the eighth of July for Shirley to finalize the wedding ceremony details. It would not have been her style to do otherwise. I say finalize because we had decided much of what we wanted soon after our engagement.

The owner of Hygeia-Ozarka Water Company was Joe Stanley, a graduate of Tech, and he made a special effort to help any of his employees who were Tech students. Soon after learning of my upcoming marriage, he called me into his office. We discussed the negative aspects of night work when starting a marriage. I was offered full time work for him during the time after marriage and until the start of the fall semester. Once classes started, he would allow me to arrange duties at his company to fit with my class and study schedule.

What a God send! The negative aspects of a drop in my income would be minor compared to the benefits to Shirley and me having some normality in our nights and days. Mr. Stanley's offer was also a great help to my dreadful grade point average. Shirley was delighted when I called and relayed the good news.

Except for one summer between my third and fourth year at Tech, I worked exclusively for Mr. Stanley. That one summer I worked at an agricultural chemical plant. Fearing for my health, Shirley implored me to reduce my exposure to toxic insecticide dust.

There is a reason why that particular summer is not referred to as being between my junior and senior years. With work and dedication, I was able to complete four years of college credits in a mere five years!

Daddy, Mother, me, Shirley, Annie, George
(July 8, 1958)

Chapter 6

Lubbock

By the power vested by The State of Texas, the Reverend Byron Howard Baldwin pronounced his son Robert Howard Baldwin and Shirley Ann DeLozier to be husband and wife during the afternoon of July 8, 1958. Standing at the altar of the Summerfield Baptist Church that Tuesday, Daddy presented us to about one hundred family and friends as Mr. and Mrs. Robert Baldwin.

Choosing Tuesday the eighth was done to maximize time off from work. Shirley's last day of work in the gas company's Hereford office was on Thursday the third. With Friday the fourth being a holiday; we had just ten days to: make last minute wedding ceremony plans, have a very brief honeymoon, move ourselves into a just rented small one bedroom apartment located on Sherman Street in Lubbock, and both of us be at work by 8:00 am on Monday the 14th—Shirley at the Lubbock office of the gas company and me at the water company. It is not surprising with so little time our honeymoon consisted of just one night in Roswell, New Mexico—not exactly the most romantic of locations. We did not care; our future beckoned.

***

Much of my memory of our college years has faded into a haze of days of little money, difficult course of study, hard work, and the wonderful discovery of each other. We resided in three different locations during that time. Our second address was 4605 'A'

Belton. It was a much larger apartment complex in a better neighborhood. A small two bedroom house on Thirty-Ninth Street was where we lived the final two years.

***

No narrative of our stint at Tech would be complete without mention of the struggle to complete the required twelve semester hours of English. I have always been, and still am, a poor speller, and my reading aloud was an excruciating experience for both listeners and me. When reading to myself if the meaning of a word was known I had no problem, and my vocabulary compared well with peers. Only in elementary school was I tested directly for an ability to spell and read aloud. So once past the early grades, I was able to work around my limitation. A better than average memory was helpful. However, my poor spelling came back to haunt me upon entering college.

I flunked the English entrance exam. Dr. Bumpass was my teacher for the remedial course. It was a composition course. Three misspelled words on a theme was an automatic F. Dr. Bumpass said to me when returning a third consecutive paper with a big red F at the top, "Mr. Baldwin, your writing may be insightful if I could ever get past your first paragraph before encountering three misspellings. Perhaps you should consider purchasing a pocket dictionary."

This I did, but not soon enough to get a passing mark from Dr. Bumpass. That little dictionary helped me complete the remedial course with my second attempt. My success was short lived as I flunked the entry level English course twice. I got it behind me in the fall of fifty-eight, our first semester after marriage.

"Mr. Baldwin," the professor queried near the end of the first meeting of my next required English course.

I sheepishly said, "Here."

"Please see me before you leave."

She was seated at her desk as I approached and asked, "Yes?"

"Mr. Baldwin, apparently you do not know the meaning of the word *classification*, because you checked *Junior* on your class ticket."

"I have sixty-eight semester hours of credit."

"Why have you waited until your third year to take freshman English?"

"I have taken an English course every semester, but I've had difficulty getting passing marks."

"Do you really think you can get a college degree without a demonstrated ability to express yourself clearly and correctly when writing?"

"I came to Tech to get a degree, and I will."

"We will see."

I earned a C minus in her class, and she wrote a nice personal congratulatory note.

The word dyslexia was not known by me until adulthood. While never tested, it seems to be the most likely explanation of my life-long problem with spelling and reading aloud.

***

By the fall semester of 1958, I was enrolled in third year level courses in my major of mathematics. Classmates in third level or higher courses were mostly people majoring or minoring in that discipline. These higher level classes seldom had more than twenty students, as compared to possibly fifty in entry level courses. As I entered the room for the first meeting of Mathematics 331, Applications of Calculus, I spotted a face which looked familiar. Approaching the desk at which he was seated, I inquired, "Do I know you?"

"You should, we have been classmates at least three times."

This was my introduction to Darrell Boyd. Darrell became my best friend from the undergraduate years. We had much in common: same major and minor, married to working spouses, plans to teach in secondary schools, active in sports and possessing a gentle nature. Our most glaring difference was Darrell's reserve compared to my lack of such. He introduced me to golf and tennis. We studied and socialized together. The socializing continued for a life time—sometimes close in time and space and at times infrequent and from a distance. But the contact was always there. The crossing of Darrell's and my paths would prove to be a seminal moment in my life which I will clarify in a later part of this book.

***

Shirley's brother Lee enrolled in Tech after his graduation from high school. He lived in a dormitory on campus, but was a frequent visitor in our house. Shirley and I did not have a washer or dryer. So our laundry was done at a coin-operated public facility. Doing the laundry was part of my household duties. After Lee came to Lubbock, we would go to the laundromat together. I was once in the same class with Lee. I'm not sure what the subject was. Perhaps it was English since after my first year most all of my English classmates were my junior by one or two years. Whatever the subject matter, Lee came to the house one afternoon for us to study together. He brought two cigars saying, "Just what we need to help our mental focus."

Wrong! In less than thirty minutes, I was hanging on the clothesline pole in the back yard throwing up. When it came time to pick Shirley up from work, Lee had to go and get her. If I had not been so ill, Shirley might have been upset when they returned.

***

The mailman delivered an envelope in mid-January 1961 with a return address of the Selective Service. The arrival was just after the start of our last semester before graduating. The letter inside gave a date upon which I was to report for physical and mental testing for possible induction into two years of compulsory military service. I could have applied for a student deferment, but the law required the request be made prior to receiving a notice for the physical examination. Shirley and I considered obtaining a deferment soon after marriage, but getting the deferment would have increased my upper-end eligibility age from twenty-seven to thirty-five. We decided not to seek the deferment.

If I were drafted, she would move back to Hereford and work while I served the two years. Then we would return to Lubbock and finish our undergraduate studies. It never occurred to us the possible interruption might be in the last term just before obtaining a degree. We talked to the head of the draft board in Hereford. She scolded us for not asking for the student deferment according to the statutes and indicated it was almost a certainty my name would be at the top of the list before our May graduation date.

A solution was offered. When I received the actual induction notice, we could then write a letter to the board and request a delay of the date to report. Being a last semester senior, the board would be apt to delay the entry date. We would wait for the induction notice and make the best of an unpleasant situation.

We stopped looking for a teaching position. No official letters came during the last of January or all of February and March, so by mid-April we contacted the woman at the Hereford draft board again. She had good news. There had been an unexpected number of volunteers, and it looked as if I would not be called anytime soon. A teaching job could be located, and as a mathematics and science teacher, I would be excused from military service if not at war.

That night we resumed our search for a teaching job. Mathematics and science teachers were in demand, and we had a plus as our academic major was mathematics, not education. I had taken education courses as electives. We could choose where to live with a high probability of being hired. Shirley and I both possessed a spirit of adventure, so going somewhere new was appealing. I'm not sure which of us suggested Colorado, but whomever, the other eagerly agreed. I had never been to Colorado, and Shirley only once during her senior trip. After obtaining a map at the nearest service station, we selected the school districts to which my resume would be sent. Our graduation gift to each other would be a trip to the selected locations for an inspection and perhaps getting an interview.

***

I walked across the temporary stage set up in the Lubbock Municipal Coliseum on May 29, 1961, to receive a diploma affirming Texas Technological College had conferred upon Robert Howard Baldwin a degree of Bachelor of Science. The next day Shirley and I headed to Colorado. We had arranged for four interviews. One was with the Huerfano School District Re-1 in Walsenburg. Walsenburg is located near the eastern slopes of the Rocky Mountains—north of Trinidad and south of Pueblo. A short, steep, and winding drive to the west led to the La Veta Pass at an altitude of just over 9400 feet. The pines, aspens, and mountain streams were beautiful.

John Mall, the superintendent, finished our interview by taking Shirley and me to the third-floor classroom of the red-brick high school building where I would conduct class if we agreed to his offer. His secretary would prepare a contract for signature that day. Looking at the magnificent view of the Spanish Peaks from the classroom windows made us want to say *yes*, but we knew it was best to go ahead with the other interviews and consider all options. We received an offer from each school district visited. All the salaries were near the same.

Back in Lubbock, we decided on Walsenburg and signed the contract on June fifteenth for a salary of $4,100. The amount later was increased by $200 for coaching freshmen boys' basketball and assisting with junior high football.

From the beginning Shirley had said she was quitting the gas company the day after our graduation. She pushed it back to a week or so before our move to Colorado. I, of course, worked at the water company until just prior to moving from Lubbock. The first day for teachers to report was August twenty-six. We planned to make a brief house hunting trip in early August and make the actual move three or four days before the starting date.

***

I received a telephone call from the superintendent of schools in Loop, Texas sometime in early July. He indicated his district was in need of a high school mathematics and science teacher and had talked to the head of the Education Department at Tech and was given my name. I told him of the contract with the Huerfano School District.

"Teachers often break contacts. You owe it to yourself for you and your wife to come to Loop and see what we have to offer."

Shirley and I talked and decided it would not hurt to go. An appointment was made for the next Saturday. Loop was a rich oil field school district. The high school was new with well-equipped classrooms. There were less than 100 students in the high school. I would be teaching all the mathematics and science courses. The salary offered was more than the signed contract, and Loop provided free houses for teachers. The houses were not very good. In fact Shirley rated them just barely adequate. The sand hills of Loop could not compete with the scenery of Walsenburg. The financial advantage of Loop made it very attractive to us. We decided to seek input from Daddy.

"Son, it is true teachers often do break contracts, but you and Shirley need to seriously consider if ya'll want to start your professional career by walking away from a commitment."

It was back to Walsenburg to find a place to live.

Mr. Mall agreed to help us. There was only one other new high school teacher that year, so it did not seem strange he would get personally involved in finding housing. We would soon find his involvement would have more to do with the lack of housing than the number of new teachers.

Walsenburg had been a mining town. Most of the mines had been closed for years, resulting in a very bleak economy. It was not much more than a pass-through point for vacationers, and a high percentage of the population was on some type of government assistance. It had been a long time since there had been any new construction. It did not take long for Mr. Mall to show us the two houses which were available. Both made the Loop housing look good, and neither one met Shirley's standard of adequacy. Noting our long faces, he said, "Let's have some lunch, and I will make some telephone calls."

Mr. Mall was not with us while we ate. After rejoining us at the café, he was reassuring. But he gave no hint of what he had in mind. Soon a man came into the café and approached our table and introduced himself. His name was Louis Feiccabrino, the owner of an electrical contracting business. With the superintendent in tow, he drove us to his house. It was a large, red-brick structure with large living and dining areas and three bedrooms. The kitchen was spacious with a breakfast nook and had the only electric garbage disposal in town. There was a full basement with a finished bedroom, bathroom, and game room with a pool table. The basement also had an unfinished work area. Built during the mining heydays, it was well constructed and had been completely updated. It sat on a large lot between the post office and the home of the president of the local bank.

"What do you think?" Louis addressed Shirley.

"It's wonderful."

"You want to rent it?" he asked.

I said, "I don't think we can afford it."

"You may be surprised. We just might be able to work out an arrangement beneficial for all."

He then told us about his situation. He had life-threatening asthma, and the doctor had advised him to relocate to a different climate. The Feiccabrinos would be moving to Arizona. They hoped it would be temporary—maybe a year or two. They loved their house and all the improvements and planned to live in it again. The thought of leaving the house vacant was not appealing, nor did they want to rent it to just anyone. We were the type of renters for which they had been looking. A young professional couple with no children or pets who would agree to take care of the house in exchange for a low rent rate.

As we were checking out the house, they were evaluating us. Ann, Louis' wife, was determining if Shirley was a person who would be apt to give the house good care. Shirley must have passed her test.

"Tell us what you can afford and we will see if it is a possibility," Louis advised.

Shirley and I went to another room to talk in private. We wanted to be fair, but our budget was tight. I do not remember what the exact amount was, but I do know it was more than what we had planned to pay but considerably less than it should have been.

They accepted our offer without hesitation. Shirley and Ann became lifelong corresponding friends. Ann complimented Shirley on how good the house looked each time the Feiccabrinos made a return visit to Walsenburg. The Feiccabrinos also left some furniture to prevent the house from looking bare.

Shirley did not spend all her time taking care of the house. She became quite good at pool by practicing during the day and beating me at night after supper. It was good, inexpensive entertainment.

Chapter 7

Walsenburg

Shirley's and my contentment levels with the year in Walsenburg were different. Oh, how we both loved the non-school hours: evenings, weekends, and holidays. Pleasant memories to be revisited throughout our marriage were: times in front of the fireplace on a cold snowy day or night, Friday afternoon trips to a mountain stream for a rainbow trout cookout, hours in the basement game-room playing pool, and weekend excursions into the high mountain valley just over La Veta Pass. However, our separate experiences during the hours of the school day were poles apart.

Give Shirley one close friend, books to read, time for hand crafts, contact with family, a house to decorate, a kitchen equipped for gourmet cooking, and a spouse (later a daughter and grandchildren) with which to share it all, and she was happy. She had all these while we were in Colorado. The wife of the bank president and Shirley became dear friends. Her last name was Murray. I do not remember her first name, and that fact would disappoint Shirley if she were here. The two of them would exchange recipes and household hints over long talks with much laughter while having a second cup of coffee. Mrs. Murray introduced Shirley to the town and its residents. Both houses had large front porches, and during nice weather, they would sit on one of the porches and holler greetings as people came and went from the post office. Some would join them on the porch for a while.

Poor economic conditions of the region elevated teachers to a higher status in the social hierarchy than normal. We both enjoyed the respect given us by the community. A positive manifestation of Shirley's comfort level with life came near the end of the school year when she expressed her readiness to be a mother.

***

During the school hours I traveled in a dissimilar, parallel universe. My first year of teaching was divided into three unique periods of time, each with its own emotional state—desperation, adaptation, and satisfaction.

Within the first few minutes after students entered the classroom on day one, I knew the environment was totally remote from expectations. There was a sinking feeling in the pit of my stomach the situation might be beyond my abilities. My past experience concerning interaction between teacher and students with classroom behavior issues was of little use. During my primary and secondary school years, there were always a few students who were disruptive and willing to push the teachers to the point of needing to take some corrective actions. Even the unruly ones knew there were limits, and the limits were not set by them, and their bad behavior was seldom, if ever, physically damaging to people or property.

It was not so in Huerfano School District Re-1. The problem students in Walsenburg seemed to accept no restraint on destructive behavior. Thankfully they were few in number, but it takes only one or two bad actors per class to destroy a learning environment. Once things get out of control, border-line kids will follow the lead of the worst perpetrators. An incident during the first week of school gave me an insight into the out-of-control actions of the delinquents.

On the third floor there were seven or eight classrooms in addition to mine. There was only one other male teacher, Bob Allen, who was the varsity boys' basketball coach. Just after changing of class periods in the morning on the third or fourth day of school, I heard a major confrontation taking place in the hallway. I moved quickly to intervene. During the early sixties, the in-vogue purse carried by teenage girls was in the shape of a small rectangular box. It was hard sided, aluminum or heavy plastic, with a suitcase type handle in the center of the top.

The scene in the hallway was surreal to me. Two girls were in a serious fight. One had the other pinned flat on her back on the hallway floor. The girl on top was striking the other on the face and head using her purse as a potentially lethal weapon. Bob and I exited our classrooms simultaneously. Bob had an athletic six feet four inch body and I weighed near 180 pounds and stood six feet one.

While running to help separate them, I heard the girl on top say, "Do you give up?"

"You don't give up unless you are dead," the other said while bleeding badly.

Bob bear-hugged the girl on top pinning her arms to her sides and lifted her up where her feet did not touch the floor. I did not react rapidly enough, and the bleeding girl sprang up and attacked her adversary. She grabbed her hair with one hand and went for the eyes with the other. Bob did a pirouette to save his captive from harm. I literally had to tackle the other to get control.

Walking back up the stairs after taking the girls to the administrative offices located on the first floor, I said to Bob, "I am not sure if I can adjust to this."

"You will get used to it."

"I'm not sure I want to."

I sought Wilfred Martinez's counsel. Wilfred was a native of Huerfano County. He attended secondary school in the same red-brick building in which he now taught. He was a good teacher who was respected by fellow staff members and students.

"Most all new teachers who come here from parts of rural Texas are despondent in the beginning," Wilfred remarked as a prelude. "Robert, number one, you must have decorum in your classroom, or you will never be able to create a learning atmosphere. Unfortunately that will not happen until your meanest, toughest trouble maker physically fears you," he continued. "All the students know who that person is and are waiting to know your response when he tests you. My recommendation is you determine his identity and confront him before this happens. That act alone will speak volumes."

"Are you suggesting I handle him with physical force?"

"Whatever it takes for him to fear you."

"I would rather quit teaching than intentionally initiate aggressive contact with a student."

Wilfred's last words rang in my ears as I tossed and turned during a sleepless night: "If you don't do it, I predict you will be back in Texas within a month. Otherwise this year will be so miserable you will quit teaching altogether."

Fear works, not always; and never forever. If used without malice, it can be a tool which has the possibility of changing into mutual respect.

Shirley and I agonized over what I should do. Being an initiator of fear was inconsistent with my self-image. But it had the highest potential for the best long-term results compared to the other unpleasant options. Thus, I would step outside my comfort zone and try Wilfred's suggestion.

I had classes ranging from physics to remedial mathematics. As you would expect, the latter contained my most severe cases of discipline. Andy Archuleta was at the top of the list.

My classroom had two doors. There was a clip in the hallway just outside the door near my desk. It was used to hang the attendance card after checking roll at the beginning of each class.

The next day after placing the card for the remedial class in the clip, I did not immediately step back into the classroom. Within a very short time I heard chaos breaking out. Entering unnoticed through the other door, I went quickly and quietly to the back of Andy's desk. He was carving something in the desk top with his switchblade. I bear hugged him from behind and yanked him up from his desk. The knife skidded across the floor. While carrying Andy to the hallway, I told one of the better-behaving students to retrieve the knife and place it in a drawer of my desk. All the other students swiftly settled down, responding maybe from fear or more likely curiosity.

Once in the hallway, I turned Andy around to face me and in the process got a good two-fisted grip of the front of his jacket. Thus, I maintained physical control. I backed Andy against a slightly ajar locker door. I stared down my nose into his defiant eyes while lifting him to where his toes hardly touched the floor. Less than six inches separated our faces.

He started to say something, and I pushed him hard backward. Metal banging on metal made a very loud sound.

"Don't you say a word," I said slowly in a low, threatening tone.

He again started to speak.

I slammed him against the locker a second time with much greater force than the first while still maintaining my strong two-handed grip on his clothing. Again the resulting sound echoed down the hallway.

"Keep your mouth shut, and don't force me to remind you again!" I shouted with enough volume to be heard in all rooms of the third floor.

Andy remained silent and avoided eye contact while I told him in no uncertain terms that he would not be allowed back into my classroom unless his behavior met my standards. He waited in the hallway per my instructions while I got his things (minus the knife). After giving them to him, I told him to go to the principal's office.

From that day forward, I seldom had to raise my voice to get an unruly student to adjust his behavior.

There was another divide between the environments of my youth and of my students. It was not nearly so obvious and would prove to be far more difficult for me to comprehend. I am not sure my words will capture the crux of the difference.

I will start by relating the details of the interaction with one of my students which revealed to me the vast gap separating our two worlds. There was this nice, young man in my algebra class. He was well behaved and very intelligent. But he seemed to have no ambition to improve and make good use of his potential. Hoping I could find words to inspire him, I asked him to drop by my classroom after school.

I started by telling him my observations about his good mind contrasted to his lack of effort. In a calm voice he indicated there was no reason to exert more energy.

"Why?" I asked.

"Why should I?"

I went into a long explanation about preparation for college in order to obtain a professional career with its accompanying benefits.

"Mr. Baldwin, I don't need or want that."

"What do you mean?"

"Life for me will be fine here in Walsenburg. My father has done ok, and he didn't finish high school."

"What does he do?"

"He used to work at a service station until he got hurt, and now he cuts firewood for a friend from time-to-time."

Not wanting to be critical of his father, I was at a loss of what to say.

What he said next made me more speechless, "The government helps my mother and father, and it will also help me."

He was not unique. This mentality was the norm for a significant number of people with multiple generational ties to the region.

***

With time I adapted to the Walsenburg school environment to a point where teaching was enjoyable. Physics class was fun from the beginning. The remedial class never became my favorite, but it became a satisfying experience. My teaching skills were better suited for self-motivated students.

Shirley and I would have stayed in Walsenburg more than one year if we had not wanted to start a family. As adults without children, living in a culture where there is a high percentage of people with different points-of-view from yours was not a problem. In fact, it may have been desirable. But we preferred our children grow up in the same environment we did, so we made the decision to move back to Texas.

We obtained a position teaching at Tascosa High School in the Amarillo Independent School District for the school year starting in late August of 1962. During the summer of sixty-two, I did not work, and we enjoyed a relaxing three months in the wonderful mountain climate of Colorado.

Our house in Walsenburg (1961)

Chapter 8

Amarillo

Shirley and I learned she was pregnant in mid-summer of 1962. The doctor estimated we would become parents near the first of March. New school, new city, and future new baby created an excitement level upon leaving Colorado rivaling our move of the year before.

We settled into a small two bedroom rented house just west of Sam Houston Junior High School. Tascosa High School was a short drive down Western Avenue. The student population was much larger than in Walsenburg. A high percentage came from affluent families. I taught algebra and plane geometry the first year and then switched to physics and plane geometry thereafter. Sponsorship of the Key Club was my main extracurricular responsibility. Many teachers had second jobs, and I had a good one. I taught algebra one night a week to airmen at Amarillo Air Force Base. During two of the summer breaks I taught remedial courses, and during the other two I was accepted into National Science Foundation summer study programs. The first was at the Oak Ridge Institute for Nuclear Studies in Tennessee, and the last was an astronomy program at Sam Houston State College.

***

Four life-changing events transpired during our five years in Amarillo: Daddy died, Kristi was born, Shirley became ill, and we left teaching.

***

My brother, Eugene, was a good player on a good West Texas State College football team. The entire family was proud, especially Daddy. Daddy provided season tickets to all family members within driving distance of Buffalo Stadium in Canyon. The team had a very successful season our first year in Amarillo ending with an invitation to play Ohio University in the Sun Bowl. Of course, a large contingent of family went to the game in El Paso. The doctor had advised Shirley not to go. She would stay with her parents, and I would travel with Mother and Daddy. Shirley was very uneasy about my going, but not because of my going without her. She had a feeling something bad would happen during the trip. I told her not to worry; all would be fine.

Our seats were near the forty yard line about twenty rows up. Daddy had purchased seats on two rows so some of the family would be seated just in back of other members. My seat was behind Daddy's just off his left shoulder. Sometime just before or perhaps just after half time, Daddy turned toward me and said, "Robert, I need to go to the hospital."

There was an ambulance inside the stadium behind the end zone. I rushed from my seat running down to the railing in front of the first row. Scaling it and landing on the track below, I ran to the ambulance and told the paramedics my father was in need of help. They went into the stands and brought Daddy down on a stretcher. As they were placing the stretcher into the back of the ambulance, a man identified himself as a doctor and offered assistance.

Mother said, "Please."

After a quick check, the doctor told the driver to get Daddy to the hospital as rapidly as possible and told Mother he would meet us there. Mother and I rode in the ambulance with Daddy. Other family members went to the hospital via automobiles.

At the hospital a coronary thrombosis was confirmed. There was some good news as it was not fatal, and the doctors were optimistic.

Eugene was removed from the game and brought to the emergency room. As he entered the room, Daddy asked him if West Texas had won. Eugene reported they had by the narrowest of margins—fifteen to fourteen.

After monitoring Daddy in the emergency room for a few hours, the doctor felt it safe to move Daddy to a regular room. He did indicate Daddy would need to stay in the hospital in El Paso a night or two before moving him to Hereford or Amarillo.

The family huddled. We had planned to drive from El Paso to Hereford directly after the game, thus we had no motel reservations. We agreed Eugene should return to his team, and Mother and I would stay at the hospital while the rest went to eat and find motel rooms.

Daddy was upbeat and not in pain by the time he was moved to a private room. Mother sat in a chair beside his bed and I in one at the foot of the bed. Our conversation was in an atmosphere of mild concern, but not high tension. We talked some about the game, but mostly about how to get home and the required adjustments needed during Daddy's recovery process.

At one point Daddy asked me to hand him the urinal. When finished, he sat up in his bed to hand it to me. I got out of my chair and reached to take it from him. When my hand was about six inches from the urinal, Daddy's hand and arm went totally limp, and he fell back in the bed as the bottle of urine fell to the floor.

I ran to the nurse's station to get help. The nurse broke for Daddy's room in a dead run with me racing right behind her. Mother was holding Daddy's head with both hands. She was on her knees with her entire body on the bed.

The nurse told me to attend to Mother and take her to the hallway. The activity in and around Daddy's room during the next hour or so was hurried with many medical personnel and different types of equipment involved.

The first few minutes I stood with my arm around Mother as we watched in silent terror. Chairs were brought for us. Sitting there, my emotions changed from terror to despair and then very deep sadness. Mother's needs were a catalyst which required me to focus on her pain not mine. In hindsight, that was a good thing.

Mother's beginning cries of anguish changed to questions of desolation. "What am I going to do?" "What am I going to do?" she asked in a quiet voice of despondency. She was looking at, but not exactly talking, to me. In that hospital hallway I made promises to Mother without authority, but with confidence that my brothers and sisters (and spouses) would fulfill these promises.

Mother and Daddy had taught us from early age to take ownership of our thoughts and actions. Seeking wise counsel is good, but who *you* are and what *you* think and do is totally up to you.

Until that night, I had never had to make a truly major decision in complete isolation. During childhood and adolescent years there was family, mostly Daddy and Mother but also sisters and brothers. Now I had Shirley, but not that night. She was in her parents' rural home with no telephone. Daddy was gravely ill and Mother struggling to cope. Other family members were somewhere in El Paso, but not able to be contacted.

Mother and I were allowed to go back into Daddy's room when the hospital staff had done all they could. Daddy appeared lifeless, lying on his back with multiple life support attachments.

They made Mother as comfortable as possible in a chair beside his bed. She spoke to Daddy in gentle tones while stroking him with her hands.

The doctor asked me to accompany him to a vacant room. Once there, he closed the door and asked where the rest of the family was. When told I was not sure when they would return, he started telling me the details of the actions they had taken. Daddy's heart had stopped beating prior to the entry of the first nurse. She signaled a Code Blue and performed CPR with no positive results. By the time a doctor arrived, the only option was to open Daddy's chest and hand massage his heart. This started a weak, irregular beat that could be maintained only by mechanical means. The doctor did not know exactly how long the brain had been without oxygen, but it was greater than five minutes. The odds of Daddy retaining a pulse without mechanical support were slight. Even with support there was only a small hope Daddy would regain consciousness. I was also advised if Daddy did awaken, he would not be the father I had once known. His brain had sustained too much damage. The doctor needed me to tell him what to do next.

"Why are you talking to me without Mother's presence?"

His judgment based on past experiences and the current situation was that I was in the unique position to view all the problems and make the best decision for all—Mother, Daddy, sisters, brothers, and me. Only Mother and I had been there when Daddy's condition suddenly had gone from hopeful to dire, and the doctor believed as a loving son, Mother's future needs—physical, emotional, and financial—should now be my most important concern. I was about to take sole proprietorship of a decision which would impact the people dearest to me.

"Must I tell you now, or do I have some time?"

"Take some time, but not much."

I wanted to be alone so I inquired about a chapel. He gave me directions.

God has never communicated as directly with me as some say He does with them. It seems God mostly provides input to me via other people. Thus, my prayer was not to have complete clarity and confidence in the decisions I needed to make—only that I be loving, patient, kind, and as clear thinking as my abilities allowed. I never want to be completely confident with decisions I make. A twinge of self-doubt in most instances improves the quality of my decisions. Once a decision has been made, I don't want to expend an excessive amount of energy on useless second-guessing.

I told the doctor to remove Daddy from the life support systems. His heart stopped soon thereafter. The man who was larger-than-life to me was dead at the young age of fifty-five. The news of his death greatly affected many in the Amarillo/Lubbock area. All the broadcast and print outlets covered the passing of a beloved local educator and minister.

Mother and I comforted each other until the rest of the family returned. Our time alone increased our very special mother-son bond.

Shirley was my only contemporary confidant concerning all the details. I wish I could say it was for some high noble reason of protecting Mother and other family members from undue additional pain (as that was part of my thinking), but mostly it was to shield me. I never felt it wise to tell Mother all of what had transpired, but I did tell my siblings soon after Mother's death.

I took a long solitary walk upon arriving at the motel. It was two or three in the morning before I received the telephone call from Shirley. The news had spread quickly in the rural countryside just south of Hereford. A neighbor with a telephone had driven to the DeLozier's farm to tell Shirley. Shirley and her parents followed the neighbor home to call me. Upon hearing her voice, I cried. She told me of her love and concern. She assured me she and our baby were fine. Looking forward to our child's birth helped ease the pain of our loss.

***

Shirley and I were making the small rented house ready for our first born. All the rooms received a fresh coat of paint. The baby's room was a neutral color as we did not know the gender. I do not recall any major issues with the pregnancy, but since I was not the one carrying the child, that might be the reason. The morning of the big event I remember well.

We anticipated the day would be near the end of February. So when Shirley woke me some time about four in the morning of the nineteenth, I sleepily asked, "Are you sure?" That was not an appropriate question to ask a woman ready to give birth. Let's just say Shirley's response got me out of bed quickly. Getting me up was just the start. Once up I was nervous and excited beyond functioning, but Shirley was composed. Somehow she managed to get me settled enough that I got her to the hospital.

The delivery process was long and difficult for Shirley. There was one other man with me in the delivery waiting room. It was not his first child, and he leisurely read while I was up and down pacing. I'm not sure of the time when the doctor came and told me I was the father of a healthy baby girl. When I inquired about Shirley, the doctor indicated she was fine but tired and would need some time to recover from the lengthy ordeal she had gone through. I was advised in about an hour our daughter would be in a crib in the nursery for new babies.

The wall between the hallway and the nursery was a viewing glass. They let me see Shirley briefly. She was in pain but very contented and had held our baby before a nurse took the child for an examination and to be cleaned. I went to the glass wall in the hallway and waited to see our daughter for the first time. She was brought in wrapped in a blanket in a crib with a pink-bordered card with the words "Baby Baldwin" stuck in at the foot end. She was beautiful!

Arriving a little early left us with a few items not completed. One was the name. Shirley came up with Kristi Denise. I'm not sure where she got the idea, but I liked it. They were not names from either side of the family.

Shirley and Kristi stayed in the hospital for a couple of nights. Even that was not enough time for me to get the bassinet. We had arranged to buy a used one from a couple in our church who were moving their child into a baby bed. We had told them the bassinet would not be needed until the end of the month. Thus, they had not yet purchased a baby bed. There were to be a few nights in which Kristi would not have a bassinet in which to sleep. Annie had come to stay and help Shirley with the house and in caring for Kristi. She took the side chair of our living room set, and covered the seat with towels and a sheet. By placing the front of the chair toward the wall, that chair became Kristi's bassinet.

Bringing Shirley and Kristi home was exciting. Kristi was placed on her stomach in the chair. She was a good baby crying only if hungry or needing a change. She consumed formula from glass bottles with nipples secured with plastic screw-on rings. All of these had to be sterilized on the stove top using a covered pan designed for that use. This item we purchased weeks before. We used cotton diapers held on with safety pins made exclusively for that purpose. Shirley gave me detailed instruction on how to do it all—from preparation of formula to rinsing poop from a dirty diaper before placing it in the pail. I had night duty. After a shaky start, I became fairly proficient. Not quite up to Shirley's standards—but close.

Holding Kristi as she drifted off to sleep after her 2 am bottle was a pleasure which can only be cherished not duplicated.

***

I feared the worst when the assistant principal appeared at my classroom door and told me Shirley was on the telephone. Shirley would never call me at school unless it was an emergency. Kristi had stood up in her high chair and fallen to the floor, cutting her chin. By the time I got to our newly purchased house on Lynette Street, Shirley had stopped the bleeding, and Kristi was almost in a mood to play rather than go to the doctor for stitches. Kristi handled the suturing better than I. The doctor told me to go outside to get some fresh air when I became pale and nearly passed out.

Kristi was a pleasure and not difficult as a toddler, except for *The Incident*. On that day Shirley and I both learned we had brought a person into this world with a mind and will of her own.

Just as I walked into the house after a day at school, Shirley swooped-up Kristi and gave her a couple of quick swats on the rump as she carried her to her room. Kristi screamed and cried as if she had been beaten. I met Shirley in the hall as she was exiting Kristi's room.

"What was that all about?" I inquired.

"I told her if she did not have all her toys picked

up by the time you came home, she would get a spanking."

Kristi was seated in the middle of the clutter of toys when I entered her room. I told her to put the toys into the toy box, but her only reaction was to scream and cry louder. Just as Shirley had done moments earlier, I spanked her on her bottom with an open hand. Her response was to sit back down in the center of the room and bawl at the top of her lungs. I returned to the living room very shaken and found Shirley sobbing. If two times had not worked, neither of us thought it helpful to try spankings a third time. So we waited anxiously not sure what to do.

The intensity of Kristi's outburst decreased after a few minutes, and then she was silent. After a few minutes more with no sounds coming from her room, we heard her get up and start walking toward her door. I rushed and stopped her at the doorway, and told her she would not be allowed to leave her room until all toys had been put away. Kristi ran back to the middle of the room, sat down, and resumed screaming and crying. This cycle was repeated two more times.

Finally, instead of heading for the door after her crying spell ended, we heard her placing something in the toy box. Then another, slowly at first but as each toy hit the box, the patter of her scurrying around increased in tempo. When she finished, the little toot came into the living room with a big smile on her face as if the previous thirty minutes of hell had not happened.

From that day forward Shirley and I found expressing disapproval or taking away privileges was the best method to get Kristi's attention.

***

Throughout the years Shirley and I had always contended the first sign there was something wrong with her health was the decrease of blood circulation in her hands. Looking back, there might have been an earlier marker. When Kristi was about two years of age, we decided it time for a second child. There was a miscarriage very early in the pregnancy, soon thereafter Shirley started having the blanching of blood from her hands. We knew having a second child would have to be put on hold.

Our regular doctor was stumped concerning the cause of poor circulation in Shirley's fingers. He referred us to a doctor specializing in diseases of the circulatory system. After several months of testing, the conclusion was Shirley had Raynaud's disease. Raynaud's disease is a rare disorder which affects the arteries and limits blood reaching the extremities. In the nineteen sixties the most common treatment of extreme cases was severing of sympathetic nerves resulting in permanent dilation of the blood vessels. Shirley did not have confidence in the doctors' judgments and wisely refused to let them cut the nerves.

She began having other symptoms which were not consistent with Raynaud's disease. Joint pain and fatigue became common. Some days she could function without major difficulty, but on others days, it took all her will power just to get out of bed. We knew something major was not right, but the doctors had no clue of what was wrong. Their advice was for us to seek help in Dallas or Houston, or perhaps one of the major diagnostic clinics. All of those options required financial resources we did not have.

The only way to increase our income and stay in the Amarillo school system would be to move from the classroom into administration. I loved the classroom, and my personal opinion was that I was a good teacher. If becoming an administrator was the best path to a higher salary, then the private sector seemed the better option. Shirley and I agreed we would leave teaching even if it meant relocating from Amarillo. I sent resumes to about ten different entities, and one was to Southwestern Bell Telephone Company (SWBT).

It was the summer of 1967, and I was teaching summer school. We received a call from a man named Presley Shepard, the college recruiter in the Dallas office of SWBT. My resume had been forwarded to him from the office in Amarillo, and he wanted to interview me. Presley would fly to Amarillo from Dallas. The interview went well, and he offered me a position in the engineering department located in Houston. Most important, the starting salary was $725 per month with a good possibility of a raise after three months. I could not wait to drive home to give Shirley the good news, so I used a pay phone just outside the SWBT building. When I told her the pay amount, her response was, "Do you have to kill someone?"

"Does it matter?"

"I guess not," she said with a chuckle.

We would move to Houston as soon as summer school ended. George and Annie were very distressed that we would be taking their granddaughter so far away. Our house sold quickly. Shirley and Kristi went to the DeLozier's, and I stayed with the Boyds while finishing my teaching duties.

Kristi and Shirley

Chapter 9

Houston

What a change! A rural couple with an active four-year-old daughter moves to the city. That alone would have been a challenge. Add the facts of the wife having an undiagnosed major illness and her husband entering a new career for which he had no background or knowledge. You might question the couple's wisdom. These were the ingredients for a most interesting year.

The economy of Houston was booming. On the plus side this was the reason we got the job. SWBT was having difficulty installing facilities rapidly enough to supply the demand. The down-side was the tightness of housing. We found an apartment in Bellaire. It was on the second floor, which was not easy for Shirley.

The move had been grueling for Shirley, and the first three to four weeks in Houston she did not feel well. During that period she went outside the apartment only for visits to doctors. Therefore, Kristi was confined while I was at the office. Shirley was up to reading to Kristi and getting her lunch and snacks but not much else. From a very early age Kristi was good at entertaining herself, perhaps out of necessity. I would bring take-out food for our supper and after eating, take Kristi to a nearby park. There we would play for an hour or two until time to bathe her before bedtime.

We were blessed with access to good medical facilities and doctors. A company doctor referred us to a specialist in autoimmune diseases, and this opened the door for a correct diagnosis. It would not come until after we moved from Houston, but the tests and analysis done while in Houston eliminated possibilities and pointed future doctors in the right direction.

One thing we did know from the beginning was whatever the problem, there would be periods of flare-ups and times of remission. Thankfully, Shirley was back on her feet after about a month in the Bellaire apartment. We started the search for a house to purchase. There weren't used ones in our price range and no new tract houses finished. Our only option was to pick a floor plan from three to four model homes, and select a lot on which the developer would build. The good news was the house would be completed in a short period of time. Our new home was built in the northwest part of Houston just north of Spring Branch.

My work location was at 3100 South Main Street. There were about fifteen engineers in the group, and each was assigned a cubicle. The engineers with seniority occupied the cubicles along the outside windows. Mine was about a hundred square feet in the middle and shared cubicle walls on three sides. There were two private offices: a large one for the group-head, and a smaller one for his assistant.

The group had responsibility for preparation of budget authorization documents, equipment ordering forms, and detailed installation specifications for telephone switching systems located at a customer's premise. These systems were called private branch exchanges or PBX's. There were two engineering administration groups for Texas; one in Houston for south Texas and another in Dallas for north Texas.

In the beginning, I was a little uneasy with being referred to as an engineer since I did not have an engineering degree. This disquiet soon diminished because nearly half of the group had started as a craftsman and had been promoted to the engineering department based on their past work performance. Of the ones in the group with college degrees, most but not all were engineering majors. We college graduates had an advantage as our entry assignment was a first-level management position. For the engineers without degrees, second-level management was apt to be the maximum opportunity, and few would obtain that. Of the ones with degrees, most all could have reasonable expectations of no lower than third-level positions. My concern of being referred to as an engineer did not vanish, because my college degree major was mathematics not engineering. However, it was an issue to be addressed in the future. Just keeping my head above water that first year in Houston was enough.

I enjoyed being exposed to a whole new world. Learning the details of how a telephone network operates was fun, and I picked it up with relative ease. It did not take long for my work output to place me in good standing.

Even more intriguing than doing the day-to-day projects was my adapting to a different work environment. Moving from an adolescent-centered school atmosphere to an all-adult private-sector workplace changed my perspective. Paramount was adjusting to a more exact and rigorous evaluation system. Our son-in-law, Stephen, had a sign in his office which said something like: *You are only young once, but you can be immature your entire life.* Never having to grow up has some advantages, but it also has a down side. Being around teenagers my first six years after college resulted in my viewing life with a youthful slant. Leaving the classroom forced me to adjust this casual nature to better fit adult situations.

About four or five years after joining SWBT, I was asked if I would go back to teaching if the pay were the same as my current salary. I had to give that question some thought. After reflection, my answer was that it depended on the amount of time elapsed since walking away from the classroom. Within the first six months, I would have gone back to teaching without hesitation. After a year or so, a school district would have had to pay me more to get me back in the classroom. After being with SWBT four or five years, returning to secondary school teaching had essentially lost its appeal.

***

The day I took off work for us to move into our new house, SWBT officially announced what employees had known was in the works for some time. Texas was to be divided into three administrative areas. San Antonio would be the headquarters for the western part of the state. The positions in San Antonio would be filled primarily by personnel from Houston and Dallas. Recently-hired employees had little leverage, so we knew San Antonio would soon be our new home. Shirley and I did not mind. Our only concern was changing doctors, and Shirley's doctor in Houston calmed that apprehension.

We settled in for a short stay in our brand new house. The time was no more than four to five months. The new headquarters was to be operational before the start of school in late August 1968. Thus, Kristi would be able to attend kindergarten without interruption. Shirley and Kristi enjoyed the new house very much. Shirley was feeling well, and Kristi had room both inside and out.

There was one negative experience I remember. Santa had brought Kristi a doll one of the Christmases while we were in Amarillo. Oh, how she loved that doll, who she called *Baby Mary*. By the summer of sixty-eight *Baby Mary* and Kristi's playtime together had taken its toll on the doll. Poor *Baby Mary* had but a few strands of what had been a full head of hair. I came home from the Houston office one afternoon and found a heartbroken daughter. One of the little girls in our neighborhood had told Kristi that *Baby Mary* was ugly!

***

The last weekend of HemisFair '68 coincided with our house hunting trip to San Antonio. It was most difficult to find a motel with a vacancy. The one we had, Kristi still calls the motel from hell. It was not clean and had a large family of three-inch long water bugs who were very territorial. I don't think Shirley or Kristi got any sleep either night we were there.

We arrived at bed time Friday night. We looked at houses all day Saturday. Shirley took notes, and I snapped photos using our Polaroid camera. That night we cut the list down to about three and returned to those on Sunday. We signed the papers for one on Wahada Street before heading back to Houston late Sunday afternoon. That house became our home for the next ten years and the place where Kristi grew from a child to a teenager. It held many fond memories.

Shirley

Me (1967)

Our house in San Antonio on Wahada Street

Chapter 10

San Antonio

We thoroughly enjoyed San Antonio. It had most all of the big city amenities without the large metropolitan feel of Houston. Of the three major population centers in Texas (the Dallas/Fort Worth Metroplex, Houston, and San Antonio), Shirley and I had less exposure to San Antonio than the others. A year was not enough time for us to acclimate to the hustle and bustle of Houston. But we felt comfortable in San Antonio within a couple of months. The relocation timing seemed especially well suited for Kristi. Within the first few weeks of being in San Antonio, Kristi began her formal schooling. She was enrolled in the kindergarten program operated by the Northeast Baptist Church, located some eight to ten blocks north of our house.

At that time we had only one automobile. Thus, Shirley had no way of driving her to kindergarten. Mary Beth Price director of the church's kindergarten program volunteered to pick Kristi up the first day. When a child leaves for school for the very first time, it can be a day of mixed emotions for parents and especially so for a mother. Shirley was no exception. I was anxious to learn how it had gone, so I called Shirley soon after the scheduled time. She advised with a slight trace of disappointment that Kristi ran eagerly to Mary Beth's car, just barely saying goodbye. Shirley's letdown of the morning vanished when Kristi returned bursting at the seams to share the details of her most exciting first day of school.

Kristi's attitude toward kindergarten's first day was a harbinger of her approach to elementary and secondary schooling. She was a self-motivated student.

Shirley and I did not have to worry about her keeping up with her studies. I remember on more than one occasion when Shirley would see a light in Kristi's room as we were going to bed and find her doing school work. Seldom was it because of procrastination. Mostly it was due to the amount assigned, or more likely Kristi's desire to excel. Shirley would tell her to go to bed, and I would talk to the teacher if needed.

Kristi had an affinity for animals. I don't remember how much input I had in the decision to get a puppy. It was a black, purebred dachshund. We could have gotten the certification papers, but did not. I bet I had input when he was named *Goober*.

After he grew out of the cute puppy stage, Goober was very active. He was so full of energy when Kristi was small, Shirley or I had to be with her in the back yard when she played with him. His nice doghouse was regarded by him to be a large chew toy rather than a place to sleep. Another family might not have appreciated his hyper personality, but we three loved that dog.

***

Systemic lupus erythematosus (SLE or lupus) is an autoimmune disease in which the body's immune system mistakenly attacks healthy tissue. Lupus affects each individual differently. Symptoms are wide-ranging and can change over time. This unpredictability can make lupus difficult to diagnose. An accurate diagnosis can take months or even years to determine. For Shirley, it took about three years.

What we were told was very sobering. There was a long list of facts known about the disease in late 1968. It affected the skin, joints, kidneys, brain, and other organs. Most common for women between the ages of fifteen and forty-five, it was a disease of flares and remissions. What grabbed our undivided attention was the reduction in life expectancy. At that time for a woman diagnosed at the age of thirty, it was estimated to be less than ten years. Shirley had just celebrated her thirty-first birthday.

At the time of the move from Houston, Shirley's lupus was in a remission stage. There was no cure then and none now. Control of the negative symptoms was the therapy, and this was done primarily with the use of drugs. Shirley was prescribed steroids, mostly prednisone, in high dosage during major flare-ups. She experienced one soon after our move. For Shirley, the connecting tissues were most affected. Thus, the seriousness depended on which organ was involved. This time it was very grave as it was the tissues around the heart which became inflamed. Annie came to San Antonio to help. Shirley was in the hospital about a week. The drug therapy was not working, and Shirley's condition became very frightening. Late one evening the doctor informed Annie and me unless there was a positive change within the next few hours, Shirley was not apt to be alive at day break. It was a long, long night of prayer and concern. By morning, she was better and soon able to go home.

Our new normal was one in which Shirley had long periods of being able to do almost anything. These good times were punctuated with numerous doctor appointments, medical tests, days when every movement was painful, and occasional hospitalizations.

Life would never again be quite as good as it would have been if Shirley had not had lupus. As with most chronic major illnesses, a disease like lupus defines its victim. Shirley and I pushed-back hard, but in time she was no longer just Shirley. She was first and foremost a person with lupus. Adjusting to that fact was totally unavoidable.

***

My new work assignment was still in the engineering department of SWBT but in the special services group rather than PBX. I was ready for a change.

The ten years in San Antonio with SWBT were good. There were promotions which led to third-level management positions. Often when promoted, people will move to a more expensive house. Shirley and I did not do that. We liked our house and did some upgrades instead. Thus, near the end of the years in San Antonio, we were incurring first-level house expenses while receiving third-level pay. A mustard-colored Fiat 128 with a checker-board vinyl top was my work transportation. The purchase price was low, but it frequently needed expensive repairs. A couple of years after buying the Fiat, we traded in our Chevrolet Biscayne for an Oldsmobile 98. This bothered Kristi a bit since the Biscayne was purchased while we were in Amarillo, and she considered it to be part of the family.

Situations can change without your realization. There was an on-the-job incident which helped me understand we had made financial advances without being completely aware of it. It happened near the end of our San Antonio years. I was supervisor of about 200 employees in four different work groups. One consisted of about ninety keyboard operators who entered equipment assignments into a data base. There was a work rules dispute which my first and second levels of management were unable to resolve. At the end of the successful grievance meeting in my office, the union representative was the last to leave. She was a single mother of three children. I had a picture of Kristi on my credenza. It was a school picture from late middle school or early high school.

"Mr. Baldwin, may I ask you question?"

"Sure."

"Is that a picture of your daughter?"

"Yes it is," I said in a proud father tone.

"How does she feel being rich?"

By her tone and facial expression, I could tell the query was sincere and without malice.

I hesitated before replying, "I don't think she looks at herself as being rich."

We did not have to be rich for Kristi and me to enjoy going to concerts. Her ninth birthday present was tickets for her and three or four friends for an Osmond Brothers concert on Friday, February 11, 1972, in the HemisFair Arena. I was one of the few dads in the arena. Mostly it was mothers with two to three young girls in tow. The arena was packed. When the opening groups finished, the arena went black, and flashbulbs popped and the screaming began. The Osmonds were on stage and singing when the spot-lights came back on. I know they were on stage as I could see them, but only assumed they were singing since it was impossible to hear anything above the ear-piercing sound from thousands of young female fans. Kristi and her friends were also in full-voice.

When the concert was over, I chased after the girls as they followed rumors the brothers had been spotted in various locations in or just outside the arena. It was all I could do just to keep them in sight. It would have been useless for me to tell them those boys were long gone by the time the house lights came on. The birthday party group didn't get much sleep that night with all the giggling, singing along with the playing of the brothers' latest album, and doing an in-sync dance step used by the Osmonds.

***

A brochure was placed in my inbox one day in the summer of 1969. Trinity University's engineering department had put together a plan which would allow people working full time to obtain a graduate degree. Shirley and I considered it to be worth a try if the school of engineering would accept a person whose undergraduate degree was in mathematics, and also if SWBT would be supportive. My supervisors were encouraging. The company would pay the tuition costs—Trinity was one of the most expensive schools in Texas—and would give due consideration to my work assignments. The dean of the engineering school granted me provisional admission with two conditions— score in the top fiftieth percentile of the engineering section of The Graduate Record Examinations, and have a mark of *B* or better in the first course of the study program. I exceeded these two requirements.

In March of 1974 I adequately satisfied four Trinity engineering professors of my proficiency in the area of engineering economy during a four-hour comprehensive oral examination. This was the final step to fulfill the requirements for Trinity University to confer upon us the Master of Science Degree with a major in engineering science. We received the diploma on May 12, 1974. In July of that year the Texas State Board of Registration for Professional Engineers completed a review of my qualifications and granted me a Certificate of Registration (Serial Number 36780) which authorized me to practice as a Professional Engineer.

***

I was born with a passion for sports as a spectator as well as a participant. I tried most everything to which

I was exposed, and I did well as a fan but was marginal as a player. Nevertheless, there were two sports at which I performed better than average—handball and long distance running. I was introduced to handball my first year at Tech. Running did not become an interest until near the end of our time in San Antonio. In fact, it was handball which got me into the streets to run.

SWBT's main administration building in San Antonio was directly across the street from the downtown YMCA. I played handball there during lunch hours. The downtown Y was a hotbed for some top handball players. There were two indoor courts where no racket ball was allowed. It was an unwritten rule that Court #1 was reserved for the better players. A newcomer had to prove himself with his play on Court #2. Imagine my delight when one day a fourth player was needed on Court #1, and I was asked to play. I substituted often but never made the list of regulars for the Big Boys' court.

The downtown Y hosted an annual handball tournament which drew the top players from surrounding states and northern Mexico. It began on a Thursday and ended the following Sunday. Players were seeded into a single elimination bracket with others near the same skill level. The first two days of competition were on courts throughout the city. By Saturday the remaining matches were played at the downtown Y. Most years I lost during the early rounds. I officiated quarter and semi-final matches during the last two days of the tournament except for one year during which I won my first five matches and advanced to the quarter-finals. My first and only match during championship weekend was against the defending Texas state champion for the fifty-and-up age group. I was then in my thirties. It was not a real match since I scored only two points in the first game and a single point in the second. He ran me all over the court while he hardly broke a sweat. I lay flat of my back in the vestibule just outside the court trying to catch my breath while perspiring profusely. When my opponent approached, he said, "You have the potential to be a good handball player if you master a lob serve and get in shape."

I replied, "I work out regularly and play handball two to three times per week."

"Do you run?"

"A little on the indoor oval above the weight room."

"Unless you do more than thirty miles per week, your heart and lungs will never be in a condition to compete in handball at a high level. Buy some running shoes, and hit the streets instead of a small indoor track." With the purchase of a pair of Etonic Street Fighter running shoes and Jim Fix's book on running, I took the first step toward becoming a runner.

There was also something which occurred soon after the handball tournament which became a part of my running legacy. Bob Schneider was a fellow employee at SWBT. He was about seven or so years my junior, a good friend, and my tennis doubles partner. We would play about once a month against Bob's twin brother and his partner. The matches were very competitive and yet fun. I told the tennis group about my recent handball opponent implying I was not in good shape. Bob's brother was a coach and physical education teacher, and he stated that a man my age in top physical condition should be able run two miles in less than fifteen minutes. I was reasonably sure I could do it—Bob didn't think so, but was sure he could do it. We made a do-and-don't bet. If I won, Bob would mow my lawn for one month. If Bob won, I would do his laundry for a month—Shirley could not help. I was not worried because I would lose only if I did not break the fifteen minute mark, and Bob did. My time was fifteen minutes and seven seconds. I don't remember Bob's exact time but it was a few seconds less than fifteen minutes. Neither of us was pleased with how difficult it was to run two miles, so we both hit the streets as running buddies.

We improved, and within a few months we were running five to ten miles at an eight minute per mile pace. The McAllister Freeway was scheduled to open on Tuesday, February 7, 1978. Bob and I did a long run on the Saturday before, starting at Interstate 410 and Broadway. We ran down Broadway to Hildebrand and then to the McAllister Freeway. Running down the middle of the north bound lanes of the freeway from Hildebrand to Loop 410 was an interesting feeling. To this day, whenever I am driving that stretch of road, I think back to that cool February morning.

***

Kristi and her grandfather DeLozier bonded soon after her birth in Amarillo. As a child, she loved to go to the farm. George would place her on his lap while driving the tractor. She would also ride in the pickup with him during trips to change irrigation water. Possibly best of all was when he let her gather the eggs from the hen house. Living in Houston and San Antonio decreased our time of being with George and Annie, but the relationship remained close.

George's health began to fail in Kristi's early teen years and became critical in the fall of 1977. Shirley drove the Oldsmobile to the Hereford hospital to be with her parents on Monday, October 24, while Kristi and I remained in San Antonio. Shirley called soon after seeing her dad and talking to the doctors. She said

Kristi and I should plan to come to Hereford. Kristi was ready to leave when I got home from work on Friday afternoon. I had packed the night before and quickly changed from suit and tie to jeans and golf shirt. We loaded the Fiat and headed north by about 6pm. Kristi finished doing some homework which was due on Monday and reclined the back of her bucket-seat and went fast asleep. It had been a stressful, busy week for her, and she was exhausted.

I stopped to get a bite to eat about nine. She did not awaken when I called to her. I reached over and shook her with my right hand, and she still did not respond. I panicked! It was a cold night, and I had kept all the windows and outside vents closed. With her lying back, I feared carbon monoxide had entered the car. I jumped out, leaving the driver's side door ajar, and raced around the car and opened the passenger's door. The cold, north winds awaked her almost immediately! She was fine.

George had congestive heart failure, and he would not last much longer. But the human body is an amazing thing. At times it can be very fragile and yet keep functioning. We decided Kristi and I would return to San Antonio. As I left his hospital room on Sunday, I was almost certain it would be the last time to see him alive. He died the next Tuesday, November 1, 1977, at age seventy. Annie sold the farm soon after George's death and moved into a new house with three bedrooms and two baths at 314 Fir Street in Hereford. She was just a few blocks west of Mother's modest two-bedroom, single-bath home on Western Street. Mother had her house built after Daddy's passing.

***

Southwestern Bell Telephone Company (SWBT) was one of the seven regional telephone companies owned by American Telephone and Telegraph (AT&T). AT&T operated the networks which handled interregional and international connections. They also controlled research, development, and manufacture of most all equipment via Bell Labs and the Western Electric Company. All the entities combined were referred to as the *Bell System.*

Transferring personnel to other locations serviced by SWBT was common. It was unusual to progress to upper levels of management without a staff assignment with the parent company. Our being at the same location for ten years and advancing from first to third level management was an exception. Therefore, Shirley and I were not surprised when I was called to my supervisor's office and told the company had a new assignment for us, and it would not be in San Antonio. We had a choice of the location—which was very rare. One was a position in the AT&T headquarters in New York City, and the other in the Bell System Center for Technical Education (BSCTE) located in a western suburb of Chicago. I had attended two classes at BSCTE and knew the work and living conditions would be very nice. Also one of the most knowledgeable doctors dealing with issues facing lupus patients was located at the teaching hospital associated with Northwestern University. Therefore, the greater Chicago area was our selection.

Shirley and I were excited about the move but Kristi not so much. She had just finished her freshman year at MacArthur High School, and the thought of changing schools and leaving friends did not appeal to her. The BSCTE assignment was scheduled to be for two years, after which we could return to San Antonio if we so desired. But Shirley and I wanted to live near Chicago at least three years to avoid Kristi having to change high schools for a second time. We had no idea it would be fourteen years before we would live in Texas again.

Kristi in driveway of Wahada Street house

Kristi in bluebonnets on Hwy 1604

Janie and Shirley

Chapter 11

Naperville

It is December 18, 2013, the day before my granddaughter Addie's nineteenth birthday. The time is 4:25pm. I know the time by looking at the clock hanging on the wall to the right and above my keyboard. The clock was given to me upon our departure from the training center located in Lisle, Illinois. Lisle is a western suburb of Chicago. The inscription on the clock reads as follows:

B. S. C. T. E.

R. H. BALDWIN

DISTRICT MANAGER-INSTRUCTION/DEVELOPMENT

PDOTS – EXTENSION DEVELOPMENT

1978 – 1981

Kristi graduated from Naperville North High School in the spring of 1981. Naperville was a seven-mile drive from Lisle, located on the outer edge of the Chicago suburbs. In fact, our new house was one-half block from the corn fields covering the land between the western boundary of the greater Chicago metropolitan area and the town of Aurora to the west.

I was one of seven district third-level managers recruited from the Bell System and transferred to the center to participate in the PDOTS training project. PDOTS was an acronym for Planning, Development, and Operation of Telephone Systems. We were to develop a comprehensive course designed for degreed engineering department employees with about one year of service and who possessed a high potential for upward mobility. The final product was twelve weeks of intensive classroom and casework training. In addition to the development, the design team of seven was also to teach the first two sessions making corrections, additions, and changes as needed. The ongoing teaching would then be handled by first and second level personnel. My area of expertise on the project was network planning. Our time frame and budget allowed for the project to be completed in two years or less.

During our remaining year in Naperville, I led the group which had oversight for course development being performed by other Bell System entities. This position required extensive travel within the United States.

***

While in Naperville, Shirley became a close friend of the woman who lived directly across the street. Her name was Sally Steinkamp. Sally loved to go, and she and Shirley did. Thus, in a short period of time, Shirley became very knowledgeable about Naperville and the surrounding area. Sally was sensitive to Shirley's illness and made accommodations for it. The result was a mutually beneficial relationship.

Our doctor in San Antonio had made arrangements for an appointment with Dr. Frank Schmid at the teaching hospital associated with Northwestern University. Becoming one of his patients was fortuitous. Dr. Schmid was on the leading edge of treatments for lupus. For the rest of Shirley's life, many of her doctors were students of, or recommended by, Dr. Schmid. Ten years had now passed since Shirley's diagnosis. She had exceeded the life expectancy of most lupus patients, and her quality of life had been better than we had anticipated. This was due to improvements in therapy medications and techniques, having informed doctors, and her being a good patient. Her activity level while living in Naperville was about the same as the San Antonio years. I recall Shirley required hospitalization only two or three times during the three years in Naperville, and none of these became life threatening.

***

Kristi was young enough when we moved to San Antonio that her memories of living in Amarillo and Houston were limited. San Antonio was the city she knew. The change of environments required adjustments not realized by Shirley and me. Students in her San Antonio elementary school were from middle income families with a mixture of white and blue collar employees. Parents with college degrees comprised less than thirty percent. During Kristi's middle and high school years there were more diverse student populations. Families ranged from high-middle income to those on public assistance.

I suspect Naperville was a small cultural shock. Naperville North High School students were more homogeneous. Their families were more affluent, and a large proportion had college educations with advanced degrees being common. Not only did Kristi adjust, she thrived. She made friends and good marks. During her senior year she applied for and was accepted for admission to the University of Illinois. Instead she chose Texas Tech. This pleased Shirley and me.

The winters of Chicago may have required Kristi's greatest adjustment, which was also true for Shirley and me. Kristi's bedroom was on the north side of the house and the greatest distance from a just-barely adequate furnace. Ice formed on the walls of her room as well as the double pane windows.

It was very difficult to keep ice off the step just outside the front door. Shirley would wait by the door to see Kristi off to catch the school bus. If icy, Shirley would say, "Be careful." After being warned and yet falling a few times, Kristi told her mother to stop the warnings as they seemed to increase the chance of a fall. One time when Kristi hit the ice and went down very hard with books and papers flying, Shirley asked, "Are you hurt?" As Kristi got herself up and retrieved her scattered things she replied, "Of course I'm hurt!"

***

There was one very sad event soon after we arrived in Naperville. We stayed in an apartment complex near the Bell System center until our furniture arrived. We arranged for our dog, Goober, to be transported via air. Bringing him with us in the car with overnight stays was not a viable option. Kristi and I retrieved him from the air cargo terminal upon his arrival. Goober seemed a little spooked, but happy to see faces he knew. An apartment was not the best arrangement for him. However, we were to be there just a few days, and Kristi played with him during my work hours, and I took him on a long run each evening. On these runs I controlled Goober by using a twenty-foot leash.

One day Kristi and I took Goober over to our new house to show him the backyard. Kristi and Goober ran and played for a short period of time. One of our new neighbors saw us and came over for introductions. We were standing in our driveway. Kristi was on my left, and Goober was sitting next to her. After a bit of small talk, the new neighbor said, "What is your dog's name?"

Kristi replied, "Goober."

The man turned and took a step toward Goober, and said, "Hey Goober" while stretching out his right hand to pat Goober on top of the head. Without warning and with a lightning reflex, Goober went for the man's throat. Goober missed the neck but did catch the man on the left part of the chin. The wound was severe. Kristi took Goober to the back of the house. I stopped the bleeding as best I could and took our neighbor whom we had just met to an emergency room for stiches. The man was very understanding.

As required by law, we took Goober for rabies quarantine. Kristi and I then returned to the apartment and explained to Shirley why we were gone for so long. All three of us were shaken and upset. We were also shocked because Goober had never shown any tendency toward viciousness. Kristi and Shirley both shed tears. I said to Kristi, "You know what this means, don't you?"

"Yes, Dad I do. Do what you must but please don't ever tell me," she sadly answered.

Sobbing, Shirley said, "The same for me."

I honored the requests, and do not believe I will be breaking a promise by revealing one thing. Before going to get Goober at the end of the quarantine period, I put on my running gear, picked up Goober, and then drove to a large open field in a rural area. There Goober and I ran together, but this time there was no leash. For the first time in his life, Goober had no fence or tether to contain him. He ran, explored, and stopped to sniff in a hurried, circuitous path and pace. I stayed with him as best as I could. When exhausted, Goober came and sat at my feet. I scooped him up in my arms and carried him back to the car.

***

The apex of my passion for running came during our time in Naperville. I had started serious running to improve my physical condition. In the beginning it was not much fun and required much willpower. I saw it as a means to an end rather than an end unto itself. My attitude about running was directly proportional to my state of conditioning. Running was painful and a chore if I was not in shape. Each small increase in my heart and lung power resulted in a tiny drop in the effort to put one foot in front of the other. Within a few months my body did not hurt while running. Instead, it felt good. When I reached that state, running became a time of pleasure and mental therapy. It also was an arena in which I was athletically competitive. I was certainly not world-class, but if I chose races carefully, my finish place was among the best of my age group. Lastly, and perhaps most important, running gave me an insight into a small but significant life mystery. In the next paragraphs I will attempt to give an understanding of why these aspects made running such a delight. Before I begin, let me again state these benefits were not realized until I reached a high level of fitness. Fifty to seventy miles per week became my norm.

Except for prior to a race, I tried to do one long run (fifteen to twenty miles) each week. It was usually on Saturday morning. I would get up near five o'clock and quickly and quietly get out of the house, trying not to disturb Shirley and Kristi. Both were very supportive of my running. I seldom stretched before a non-race run. The first three to five miles were run at a slow pace allowing my body to loosen and warm up. I then steadily picked up the pace until I was running just below an anaerobic level. I would then run ten to twelve miles at that speed. The pleasure during these miles is difficult to describe. There was a sensation of gliding with my feet lightly touching the ground just long enough for a slight forward push. All parts of the body felt featherlight and functioned in effortless harmony. It seemed as if I could do it all day. If there is such a thing as a *runner's high*, that's where I was during these miles. All good things must end, and I changed things by increasing to an anaerobic level. How long I could run in this oxygen-deficient state was a function of how much I was above my anaerobic threshold. Some days I would choose to make it last four or five miles, and other times I would crank it up enough that after a mile or two my body was begging for air. In the last miles of the run I gradually decreased the pace, allowing me to catch my breath and lower my heart rate. At the end I would do some walking to cool down and then stretch.

It took me many days and road miles to know the feeling when my body was near the point of transition from aerobic to anaerobic. As the body enhances its efficiency, the point occurs at a higher running velocity. In the beginning stage of my street running, improvement was exponential. It then slowed and leveled off as I reached the fastest aerobic pace allowed by my God-given physiology. Since I understood none of this before becoming a runner, I can only guess at my beginning threshold speed. It was somewhere between nine and ten minutes per mile. At my best fitness level it was less than seven minutes per mile. My before-and-after rested pulse rate went from the mid-seventies to the low forties, and my weight dropped from nearly 200 pounds to less than 150 pounds.

I viewed my surroundings while running in ways not possible while walking or riding in an automobile. There is nothing like waking early on a winter-weekend morning to a quiet that can come only from the sound-absorbing effect of a blanket of a few inches of new fallen snow. It made me hustle to beat any early rising drivers to the neighborhood streets. I ran slap-dab in the middle of the street where I left running-shoe prints in the glistening white layer. They were the only signs of human movement until the beautiful scene was spoiled by not-so-beautiful tire tread marks. Those winter morning runs in the streets of Naperville were a close second to the runs at sunrise in the Green Mountains of Vermont during the season of fall colors in 1979.

Running was gratifying without competition, but my enjoyment was enriched by comparing performances. At first I used a previous result of mine as the standard. Most serious runners know their personal record (PR) times for various distances, and they have a feeling of accomplishment anytime a new PR is achieved. However, in all sports, I wanted to match my abilities with others. No matter what the sport was, I could find a peer skill-level group. At times I had to put my ego in check and be realistic concerning my abilities, finding a group low in the pyramid of skill levels. Running was different, and the year was 1980. It was the year of my forty-second birthday, and I was at the top of my running fitness. My performances for distances from one mile to marathons were above average for my age group. PRs during the year reflect that. I broke five minutes for one mile in the Run for the Roses Race on Mother's Day in May. My time was four minutes and fifty-four seconds. That day I was the first runner to cross the finish line and surpassed all younger runners. On three different occasions, I finished ten kilometer races in less than forty minutes. My best time was thirty-nine minutes and seven seconds in the Police Classic, an annual ten-kilometer race in Naperville.

I set a goal of qualifying for the Boston Marathon, scheduled in April of 1981. Only the marathon in the Olympics was more prestigious. The Boston Marathon was the only other marathon for which you had to qualify to be an official entry. At that time, men forty years of age and older must have completed a sanctioned marathon in three hours and ten minutes or less. In the fall of 1980 I ran the City of Lakes Marathon in Minneapolis. With a time of three hours nine minutes and thirteen seconds, a meager forty-seven seconds under the required time for Boston, I had qualified. It seemed almost surreal that three years earlier I was unable to do two miles in less than fifteen minutes, and I had just run twenty-six point two miles at an average pace of seven minutes and thirteen seconds per mile. I ran the Boston Marathon, and it was an experience never to be forgotten. My performance was poorer than I had hoped. Time has eroded the disappointment I felt back then. It is an accomplishment which I still savor.

Whenever Kristi faced issues which needed input from me, and if I had no solution, my response was, "Life is not fair." In her senior year, after having a very trying day, I asked her if she wanted to tell me what the problem was. Kristi said, "Yes, but please don't just tell me, 'Life is not fair'."

You, the reader, may wonder what this exchange has to do with the author's running. *Fair* is a powerful word. Most everyone agrees in all things, there should be fairness. But unfortunately the meaning of the word *fair* varies with the situation. Two people can have totally mutually exclusive opinions about the same situation, and both justify their points-of-view as a matter of fairness. There is a situation in running in which, by my definition, there is complete and absolute fairness. It is during the final six miles of a marathon. No one can still be running with good form after the twenty mile marker unless he has paid his dues on the roads. It does not matter how much natural athletic talent he has. Being smart, rich, or tall will not help the untrained. Those final few miles have no interest in who you know or what your family ties are. Finishing well in a marathon is reserved for the few who are well prepared, both physically and mentally, and run the race smartly. It is not heroic to crawl across the finish line. It is a sure sign of lack of training and execution.

***

Next are two definitions from the online edition of the Merriam-Webster Dictionary:

faith *noun* \\\'fāth\\ : *strong belief or trust in someone or something.*

be·lief *noun* \\bə-\'lēf\\ : *a feeling of being sure someone or something exists or something is true.*

In the King James Version of the Bible the following two passages can be found:

Now faith is the substance of things hoped for, the evidence of things not seen. Hebrews 11:1

...God hath from the beginning chosen you for salvation, through sanctification by the Spirit and belief in the truth. 2 Thessalonians 2:13

As the son of a Southern Baptist minister, I was a regular attendee of church services at least three times each week. It was an integral part of who I was. In childhood and adolescence, it was as natural to me as my blue eyes and brown hair. My belief in the existence of God and faith in His omnipotence could not have been firmer unless embedded in my DNA. That sureness was a liability. In the movie *Ordinary People* which was released in 1980, there is a scene in which the main character, a troubled teenage male, has a conversation with his soon-to-be girlfriend. They are sitting in a café booth. Part of the dialogue included the girl asking the boy if he believed there was a God. When he said he didn't, she wondered if he might believe just a little bit. He then indicated it is not a matter of degrees, either you believe or you don't. For the first time I realized I was not sure. That initiated the unravelling of my faith.

If there is an all-knowing God, there is no use trying to hide my inner thoughts, and I cannot will myself to believe that which I do not. Thus, I became a nonbeliever.

I told Shirley, and she asked, "Are you sure?" There was no desire to change Shirley or any others. In fact I avoided talking about my loss of faith especially with Christians, who included most all family members and friends. I knew their love and concern would give them pain. My life style and value system had served me well for more than forty years, so I saw no reason to change. Of course I stopped going and giving my tithe to the church. Those people that did know would ask what happened to cause me to change my belief system. I found it not easy to explain.

I suppose I should try to do so herein. It is problematic for me to reconstruct my reasoning as a boy. I doubt I engaged in much deep thinking then. Looking back, there was an item in the news which was totally foreign to me. It was the story of a young boy near my age who had died from horrific physical abuse by his parents. I could not comprehend how a father and mother could do such a thing. I did not dwell on it long, but I suspect it may have been one of many items for which one might wonder why a loving God would let such cruelty happen. At the time, it never entered my mind to question God. In college I became out-of-step with my church concerning the process God used for creation. It was more of an issue of how I viewed my fellow Christians, rather than the doubt of a divine creator. I could keep listing other events and items which might have affected my faith, but they would not serve as an explanation. It was such a slow process with numerous seemingly insignificant events. I was not consciously aware of the gradual changes in my thinking and feelings. There was no single event. One analogy which comes to mind is the change of a rock in a river.

***

The summer of 1981 was a time of adjustment. Kristi had graduated from high school and would be heading off to college in the fall. Shirley and I were about to become empty-nesters. We decided it was a convenient time to leave Naperville. I was on loan to the training center, since it was not intended to be a permanent assignment. We had hoped to return to San Antonio, but the Texas economy was in a downturn. My ex-supervisor in San Antonio advised it would be best if another short-term assignment within the Bell System could be found. I had access to the listings of all open third-level positions. Most important was to find one matching my skills and knowledge. Therefore, job duties were what I checked first. If they did not match, I turned the page without looking at any other details. Early in the search, I came across a position for which the duties seemed to be written for me. My eyes quickly moved to the box labeled *Location* in which was entered *San Juan, Puerto Rico*. I called Shirley and the possibility excited her. Without hesitation, I dialed the contact number and talked directly to Mike Ewasyshyn, the person in charge of the Bell System group on the island. I first inquired if the position had been filled; many openings were closed before the sheet was added to the binder. Mike said he had not yet found anyone with the required work experience and was pleased when I gave an overview of my experiences. Mike was flying to Detroit the next week and asked me to meet him in a restaurant in the air terminal. The meeting resulted in a job offer and my acceptance.

I was to report for duty about a month before Kristi was to check into her dormitory at Tech. The housing market in Naperville was not good for a seller, so we decided to lease ours and wait to sell. The company provided an automobile, and AT&T

encouraged employees to rent a furnished apartment. Therefore, we would sell our cars and put our furniture in storage. Weight limits allowed us to take only clothes and a few kitchen items to Puerto Rico. Shirley separated the items going with us to Puerto Rico from the ones for storage and dealt with the movers and the company which was to manage the leasing of our house. Kristi was busy getting ready for college and finishing her job with a retail store in the Fox Valley Shopping Mall. While they were hard at work in Naperville, I was living in the Howard Johnson Hotel in San Juan and getting acquainted with my new work environment.

I flew back to Chicago about a week before our move. Kristi and I loaded her stuff in the black Oldsmobile 98 and headed to Lubbock. There we moved her into her room. I sold the Oldsmobile and took a taxi to the airport for a flight back to Chicago. The next day the movers emptied our house. Shirley and I checked into a motel and sold the Fiat to a used-car lot. The next morning a taxi collected Shirley and me with our stuffed luggage. In one were Shirley's favorite skillet and sauce pan. Boarding the airplane, we were almost giddy with delight about this novel adventure upon which we were embarking.

Our Naperville house

Me 10K Oglesby, Ill
(June 28, 1980)

Chapter 12

Puerto Rico

We leased a small two-bedroom condominium with an ocean view. It was on the sixteenth floor of the Marbella del Caribe-Oeste located in Isla Verde, Puerto Rico. For the next five years we were lulled to sleep by the sound of the surf lapping upon the beach.

The organization in Puerto Rico was unlike others in the Bell System. The entity's name was *American Bell International* (ABI) and existed under the umbrella of AT&T International. Our sole objective was to provide consulting services to a single client, Puerto Rico Telephone Company (PRTC). This advisory unit had been created a few years earlier and had about forty employees. The number was about fifteen when I joined. All lived and worked on the island. The company and its employees had a level of autonomy not present in other parts of the Bell System. Of all the perks associated with the Puerto Rico assignment (and there were many), I cherished that sovereignty the most.

The client desired consultants with on-the-job experience, and our international salary bonus would be included in our pension's calculations when we retired. These two factors resulted in an older staff. At age forty-three, I was the youngest. A high percentage expected Puerto Rico to be their last assignment. That was the case for Mike Ewasyshyn, my boss.

My primary responsibility was in the area of network expansion. In addition, I would do any special projects which required engineering economic analysis. Fulfilling those duties was challenging, interesting, and very rewarding. The greatest increase in my professional abilities took place during our half-decade in the Caribbean. The work experiences for most all of my

AT&T colleagues were also positive, but not necessarily so for their spouses. Living in a foreign culture is not for everyone. A large number of the wives were unhappy. This was not true for Shirley and her best friend, Florence Scott. AT&T brought Florence and her husband, Leon (*Scotty*) to Puerto Rico soon after Shirley and me. The Scotts moved into the same high-rise. Scotty and I hit it off from the beginning, and even more so for Shirley and Florence. They could not drive because of liability issues concerning Scotty's and my PRTC-provided automobiles. The two women kidded Scotty and me saying we were just too cheap to ship a car from the states. Loss of driving privileges did not confine those two independent females to their small living quarters. They rode the city buses (called *guaguas* by the locals). Schedules were very unreliable, and the buses were old, broken down, crowded, and not air conditioned. The up-side was a price of only twenty-five cents per ride.

When not out exploring, they could sit on the balcony and talk for extended periods. In addition to a spirit of adventure and the pleasure of each other's company, Shirley and Florence shared another helpful trait for living in an unfamiliar environment. Both could be contented being alone. For them, it was not a time for depressing idleness. Among other activities, Florence enjoyed writing poetry. Shirley loved doing crossword puzzles, reading, and doing needle work. This mixture of being able to find an inner serenity and also loving to embrace the unknown was a good combination.

***

During the few days between my telephone conversation with Mike and my flight to meet him for the interview, Shirley contacted Dr. Schmid's office to get information concerning the medical situation in San

Juan. The news was encouraging. One of Dr. Schmid's ex-students was in practice there. His name was Dr. Mendez-Bryant, and Dr. Schmid's office provided Shirley with contact information, her medical records, and a letter of introduction. Shirley made an appointment to see the doctor soon after arriving in Puerto Rico. Shirley and I were well pleased with the care she received. It was necessary for us to fly back to Chicago on two occasions when Shirley required hospitalization. The ratio of good to bad days remained about the same as in Naperville.

***

In the states we added network facilities in anticipation of future customers because there was adequate plant to meet current demand. This was a trademark of telephone networks in technologically advanced countries, strived for in locations with slightly less established infrastructure, and totally unfeasible in under-developed situations. PRTC fit into the middle category. Thus, the processes and techniques I utilized in earlier work experiences were not totally sufficient for the issues facing the PRTC network planners. I needed to supplement my skills and knowledge. Personnel in the New Jersey headquarters were not helpful because their mission was to sell telephone equipment, so I looked for other sources. I was vaguely familiar with the existence of a United Nations (UN) special agency which had oversight for international telecommunications interconnect standards. This agency was the International Telecommunications Union (ITU) based in Geneva, Switzerland. It also had a unit which provided telephone plant expansion assistance to member countries with under-developed networks. ITU publications specific to my needs were available and with the assistance of a Department of State employee, I was able to obtain copies. That employee was Julia Albrecht. Contacts can be important. Although unknown to me then, Julia would play a key role in Shirley's and my future.

One ITU document piqued my interest. Not just to help me be a better consultant, but it also opened my thinking regarding opportunities outside the Bell System. The document was titled *The Missing Link*. It was the final report of an independent commission charged with identifying causes of disparities of telephone services and creating proposals to lessen such disparities. One of the recommendations contained in the document was for the formation of a new entity called *The Centre for Telecommunication Development* (CTD). It was to contain three units—policy, development, and operations. The functions listed for the CTD's development unit were in line with my background. I telephoned Julia Albrecht to learn if the new group had been formed and staffed. She informed me the basic structure had been completed, and the request for submission of candidates for the position of executive director had just been circulated. She wanted to know if I had an interest. I told her, "Not for Executive Director, but I would certainly like to head up the development unit. Please, let me know as soon as that job request is issued."

Julia then explained the process. If I wished to be head of a unit, it would be wise to apply for the executive director position. The ITU expected to receive a *curriculum vitae* from three to four hundred people. An outside private firm would be contracted to cut the list to the top fifty. Ten would then be selected for personal interviews in Geneva. After the interviews, the executive director would be named. The last two steps would involve political considerations in addition to background qualifications. Julia believed my credentials gave me a high probability of making the unbiased first cut, and if I did, my name would be known to the people making the later unit-chiefs selections. Shirley and I decided to try her approach. I applied for the executive director position, and did make the list of fifty. My work in Puerto Rico was a plus, and I also had one guest editorial and two articles published in a telephone trade magazine.

***

On January 8, 1982, Charles L. Brown chairman of the American Telephone and Telegraph Company signed a document which led to historic changes in the telecommunication industry. The legal name for the document was a *consent decree*, but in essence it was the obituary of *Ma Bell*. Chairman Brown's agreement settled a US government's antitrust case against AT&T. In exchange for the US Justice Department's termination of its antitrust lawsuit, AT&T agreed to divest itself of the seven regional operating telephone companies. My home company, Southwestern Bell, was one of the seven. Times of change can be perilous, but they can also open doors of opportunity. My assignment in Puerto Rico placed me directly in a position for one of those positive possibilities.

A low-midlevel management position was not the most advantageous place to be privy to the insights of the breakup of the Bell System. That is, unless one is assigned to provide strategic planning to an island state such as Puerto Rico. I was in the perfect place at exactly the right time, and my opportunity was hand-carried to me in a large, sealed yellow envelope by my boss, Mike Ewasyshyn.

Mike entered my office early one morning with the yellow envelope. He closed the door, and said he had a special project for me. I was to analyze the documents in the envelope for possible impact on PRTC. Mike deemed it important enough to relieve me of all other responsibilities. He also gave me the name and telephone number of an AT&T lawyer located in Washington DC and advised me to direct any questions to the lawyer. He exited my office without providing any further instructions. The contents of the envelope were confidential documents related to the soon-to-be-announced breakup of the Bell System and the ramifications associated with telecommunications deregulation. These were separate but entwined issues. I could hardly believe what the materials revealed. My head was so bell-shaped it almost rang when I walked. What could be gained by agreeing to divestiture? Had we not created the finest telecommunications network in the world? Thankfully I had a task to do, and it did not require answers to these questions. My focus must be on the client—not me.

The client would feel the rumble of a seismic change, the magnitude of which was hard to overstate. I informed Mike of my opinion. Until the government regulatory agencies issued detailed rulings, there was little exact information to guide a telephone company. Mike indicated any and all information relating to deregulation, divestiture, and privatization received by him would be forwarded to me. This responsibility consumed me. Change and adjustments became the new norm for both PRTC and American Bell International. ABI ceased to exist. It became part of a newly created entity called AT&T International-Advisory Services (AT&TI-AS). Per my recommendation, the Puerto Ricans requested a shift in the type of consultants. The need was for people with backgrounds in marketing, privatization, and new services. The total number of consultants was about the same, but the mix changed. Mike retired, and his replacement was a person with a marketing background. A good rapport with the client and detailed knowledge of the new rules and regulations were my ticket to staying on the island. A new AT&T International person arrived on the island which would prove to be the beginning of the end of our consulting contract. He came to fulfill AT&T International's primary mission—the selling of equipment. His number-one client was PRTC.

This project gave me an understanding[3] of the future for telecoms. Access to the documents and the lawyers who wrote them were not afforded many other managers of my level. While this gave me a grasp of the impact on locations with mature networks, it was not adequate for a developing country. Those skills and knowledge were developed on the job in Puerto Rico and included researching publications produced by the telecommunications agency of the UN. That process opened the door for my future.

The death of Ma Bell changed Shirley's and my life. Technically I was still an employee of Southwestern Bell (SWBT) on loan to AT&T International. We had a choice: stay with AT&T International or return to SWBT. Our selection, once made, was not reversible. We fretted. Now I can see our worry was wasted as we both loved the more adventurous path. We tied our future to AT&T International.

***

You would think with all these exciting happenings, that I would have avoided petty work-place

---

[3] Proof of the level and timing of my knowledge can be verified by reading an editorial and two articles published in the trade journal *TELEPHONY*. The guest editorial was titled *A Lesson from the Airlines* and was in the November 7, 1983 issue. Next I authored an article concerning telephone companies' adjustments needed for a non-monopolistic environment. It was published on March 5, 1984, under the title *Fighting the Bypass Threat*. Finally, I was the coauthor of the cover-story for the April 25, 1985 edition of the journal.

dramas. If that is your assumption, you are wrong. Not only was I involved; in one case I was the instigator. I was convinced that I would replace my boss, Mike Ewasyshyn, when he retired. When Henry Fogel was announced as Mike's replacement, I was crushed. It had nothing to do with Henry, since I didn't know him. After Henry and his family had moved from California to Puerto Rico, I waited until he had been on the job for a couple of weeks. Then I made an appointment to speak privately with him. After I entered his office, I asked, "May I close the door?"

"Sure," he replied as he motioned with his hand for me to sit down.

Once seated I said, "Henry, Shirley and I have been in Puerto Rico more than two years, and we think now would be a good time to relocate back to the states."

"I am disappointed but not totally surprised. I am aware of your unhappiness at being bypassed," Henry replied.

"I did not realize it showed."

"Robert, it is not just you. I know other AT&T consultants and also some PRTC personnel expected you would replace Mike."

"All the more reason it will be good if I leave. I assume you have no problem with my searching for a stateside position?"

Henry did not immediately reply to my question. Instead he rotated his chair 180 degrees and leaned back slightly as if gazing at the painting above his credenza. He stayed in that position for a few quiet seconds, and then he turned back facing me. Henry leaned forward placing both elbows on disk and said, "Robert, I want you to do me a favor. I need you to stay in Puerto Rico until I am able to establish myself with both the client and the AT&T employees. If you will do that, then I will do everything within my power to get you a stateside assignment of your choice."

I returned to my office and called Shirley to tell her not to pack.

***

While Shirley and I were living the good life in Puerto Rico, Kristi was working through the trials of obtaining her college education. Making the dean's list was common for her, and she finished her degree requirements in three years. We had felt it wise for Kristi to live on-campus and not have an automobile during her first year. She changed both situations soon after completing her first year studies. The car selection was a Chevrolet Cavalier which she called *Runt Car*, and she used it to get to and from her small off-campus apartment in the northwest part of Lubbock. Kristi enjoyed her trips to Puerto Rico, where she lounged on the beach, read, and listened to the gossip of tourist from New York City. I don't recall exactly when Shirley and I first heard the name *Stephen*, but we knew by Kristi's tone that he was important. A son-in-law seemed to be on the horizon. Kristi completing her education was our main concern. Stephen's father, Sid Williams, was the Frio County Judge and his mother, Linda Davis Williams, was a graduate of Brown University.

Shirley regretted not being with her daughter for the selection of the wedding dress. Kristi did the preliminary wedding planning with details finalized in a single weekend trip by Shirley and me to San Antonio. We flew from San Juan to San Antonio just before Kristi's big day. It was a beautiful wedding with many friends and family members attending.

***

The Puerto Ricans did not renew our contract. I was the last consultant to exit the island and had responsibility of final closure of AT&T's advice services in Puerto Rico. My last act included turning in all keys, security identification badges, and my PRTC-provided car. This happened in the summer of 1986. Henry Fogel had departed about a month earlier to his new assignment in the Basking Ridge, New Jersey headquarters. I was to report to a yet-to-be-defined position in the same location. Shirley and I boarded the airplane heading to Newark with mixed emotions. We were going into a work situation for which I had no background. I was a telephone man, not an equipment salesman. Despite the uneasy feelings, we were excited about another new beginning. Sitting on the tarmac, a thought hit me. I turned to Shirley and said, "Do you realize we have no keys? We own nothing important enough to require a lock." We had no automobiles; we had sold our house in Naperville after the market improved, and I had just given my office keys back to the client. It may sound strange, but not needing keys was a good feeling.

AT&T personnel in Puerto Rico (Henry Fogel in light coat with right hand on rail and I am just over his left shoulder. John Sepp is in the front row with his left hand on the rail)

Chapter 13

New Jersey

John and Pat Sepp came to the airport to chauffeur us to our rented apartment. John and I had worked together in Puerto Rico, and Pat and Shirley were friends. Welcome back to reality—John gave us keys to the apartment. John also advised that I had been temporally assigned to work with him on the reorganization to meet the demands of operating in a new environment of divestiture and deregulation. We were reporting to Henry Fogel. A rough draft of an overall organizational chart already had been sent to upper level management for review. The plan contained position titles without proposed names. There were fewer posts than current employees, and the gap was too large to close with normal attrition. Layoffs were part of post-divesture. John thought we were safe. Surely we would not be allowed to have input with personnel placement unless our names were there—it made sense to me.

Shirley and I had a few days to get settled: open a local bank account, purchase automobiles (our first Cadillac for Shirley and a Chevy Spectrum for me), and select a real estate agent to find permanent living quarters. Housing was expensive and tight. There was nothing near Basking Ridge, which was affordable and also suitable. Shirley found a model floor plan in a condominium complex near Sparta, New Jersey. None were currently ready for occupancy, but one would be complete within a month. We signed a contract. It was to be a long commute for me—forty-five minutes one-way on the best of days and up to two hours if a major accident occurred.

***

During our year in New Jersey, Shirley's health declined. We were not able to find a doctor with a strong background in treating lupus patients, and the illness had done damage. Also, the drugs necessary to control tissue inflammation had major negative side effects. Nearly twenty years of taking steroids had caused impairment of her kidneys. It was only after we left New Jersey that we learned the magnitude of the damage. Shirley and I had learned to cope with the negative effects caused directly by lupus. But we had not yet realized the destructive consequences of her medications. What a paradox: the drugs which helped Shirley function and stay alive were also agents of harm. The good was immediate while the bad worked in a slow insidious manner.

Shirley's quality of life was essentially a step function when lupus was the only issue. On days of remission, she could live almost as if nothing were wrong. Not the case in times of major lupus flare-ups; on those days she did not get out of bed. Her body's negative reaction to the ongoing damage done to her kidneys by the steroids was more like a gradual declining ramp. Shirley did not begin to notice the negative effects of the gradual buildup of waste products in the blood until that year in Sparta. Neither of us comprehended what was happening. We just knew something was different and felt there was a new normal to which we must adjust. It was not debilitating; she just did not ever feel well. Shirley, as usual, became close to a woman with shared interests. Her name was Sue Wilson, and she lived in the same condominium complex. Fred, Sue's husband, was my weekend tennis opponent.

***

My temporary assignment lasted only about six weeks. The main function of my permanent position was oversight of the budget. I had worked with equipment budgets back in my days in Southwestern Bell, but this was my first time to be involved with the totality of a budget for a corporation. The second-level management person reporting to me was very skilled. She was empathetic and helped me get up to speed quickly. Henry Fogel was my supervisor, and he reported directly to Walter Murphy who was a vice president. (Note: Walter Murphy was later to die in an airplane crash in the Balkans with U.S. Commerce Secretary Ron Brown of President Clinton's administration). Walter was charged with responsibility for developing AT&T's globalization strategy. There were not many headquarters employees with operating telephone company experience, so what I feared would be a liability was in actuality an asset. Part of the reason I was in Walter's group was to provide a network operations point of view.

A man outside of the old Bell System was hired as president of AT&T International. This move was part of the new thinking. His name was John Hinds, and I believe he came from an executive position with General Electric. One of Mr. Hinds' first acts was to call a vice president's level meeting to give him a detailed overview of the company and its operation. The meeting was held in Basking Ridge and lasted a week. It was a stressful time. The second-level and I were to prepare the text and overhead projector slides for the budget presentation which would be delivered by Walter Murphy. Our time slot was on the fourth day just before the lunch break. I was to be in the meeting for Walter's presentation. It was not planned for me to say anything unless Walter was asked detailed questions. Henry Fogel was also present.

While preparing the budget report, I received a telephone call from the vice president in charge of the Asian region. He and I had not met. A vice president was two levels above me. I wondered why he had bypassed the chain-of-command. He had a simple request. In the budget for local national personnel, he wanted me to report only total dollars and no headcounts. "It would give Mr. Hinds the wrong impression, if every 'tea pourer' were counted," was his rationale.

I understood the request better the next day after a call from the vice president in charge of Europe. He also voiced a request. No surprise! He wanted to be sure I used number of personnel when reflecting all budget requests. His particular desire was that our new president should know the exact headcount of local nationals employed in each region. "How else can Mr. Hinds be in a position to make a correct comparative analysis?"

Oh boy, just what I needed—to be caught in a vise with jaws made of two VP-size egos.

I was not in Puerto Rico where I had been my own boss. In Basking Ridge, I reverted back to survival skills honed in the wilds of the stratified hierarchal structure of the old Bell System. Back then, the high costs of a mistake were weighed against the low possibility of reward for actions outside traditional practices. Thus, I ran to the protective cover of supervision. I grabbed Henry and took him to Walter Murphy's office, where I told them the contents of my two telephone conversations. Walter, like Henry and me, was in no mood to get into a squabble. We tried finesse. I was told to prepare the budget report using the exact information as provided and not hide differences. But also do not make them obvious. The final stack of overhead slides was more than two inches high. Buried about two-thirds of the way down was the slide containing breakdowns by regions of local national personnel. It was a very busy slide of a large spreadsheet with lots of numbers and notes. Only a person with a quick, keen eye would spot the difference of reporting between the European and Asian regions.

The meeting was in a large conference room with a highly polished hardwood rectangular table. There were plush leather chairs on three sides of the table. An overhead projector was on the width-side of the table where there were no chairs. Walter stood at that end to give the budget report. Mr. Hinds was seated to the right of Walter in the first chair on the length-side of the table. VPs filled the other swivel chairs around the table. Along the wall facing Mr. Hinds, a row of straight-backed chairs had been placed behind the VP's chairs. Those were for support personnel such as Henry and me. The conference room's door was behind the VP seated at the opposite end of the table from Walter. I was in the straight-back chair nearest the door with Henry sitting to my right. Mr. Hinds asked pointed questions, but Walter handled them well during the first two-thirds of the report. I was proud. The troubled slide's image was on the screen briefly, and then Walter moved on. Walter flipped over two more slides before Mr. Hinds stopped him.

"Walt, there is something on an earlier slide I do not understand."

Walter put up the previous one.

"No not that one. Go back two more."

The big-bad image was back on the screen. Mr. Hinds went directly to the problem and asked Walter to explain. Of course Walter could not without putting two VPs on the spot. Walter tried to do a *soft-shoe dance* around the issue. Mr. Hinds sharply cut him off. Henry jumped in to save his boss only to receive a greater wrath. The room became hushed. Mr. Hinds stood up and in a loud voice said, "Is there anyone in this room who can explain the differences on this chart?" (I have omitted a couple of colorful adjectives from Mr. Hinds' exact quote). All heads turned and looked at me. I sat erect and tried to keep a calm demeanor, but no words came from me. It was a no-win situation, and silence was the best of bad options. Mr. Hinds said, "This meeting is over!" and stormed out the door. Henry and I followed Walter to his office. Considering what had just transpired, Walter was not so distraught. He told me not to worry and even joked about it. I knew all was fine between Walter and me, but I was not so sure about Mr. Hinds.

***

I answered my office telephone normally that Monday morning in late July 1987.

"Good morning, this is Robert Baldwin speaking."

"Hello Robert, this is Julia Albrecht from the State Department. How are you doing?"

"Fine and you?"

"Very well. The reason I called is to see if you are still interested in a unit head position in the new development group in Geneva."

"You bet I am!"

"Good, can you arrange to be in Geneva by 2pm this Thursday for an interview?"

"I will call the airlines as soon as we hang up. Do I also need to book a hotel?"

"No. The UN will handle the hotel. Please let me know your flight itinerary when you have it."

"Will do and thank you very much."

With details to handle I did not have time to immediately savor the personal satisfaction afforded by the content of Julia's telephone call. I called Shirley and then stuck my head in Henry's office and told him the news. I then hurried back to my office to call the airlines. While I was on hold with the airlines, Henry walked into my office, closed the door and sat down in one of the two visitor's chairs. He did not say a word, but I could sense it best to hang up the telephone. Henry Fogel told me he had some unpleasant information. Upper level management knew about the UN position, and they had submitted a candidate's name through formal channels. The person was not me. My heart sank. Some vice president, or an assistant vice president, had been submitted for the post of our dreams. Sometimes, life really is not fair.

As Henry got up to leave my office, he dropped the bomb shell. He said, "The candidate is me." He hastily exited before I could think—much less talk. I sat in stunned silence for a moment.

"Wait just a cotton-picking minute!" I said aloud to myself. I made a bee-line to Henry's office. Closing the door but not taking time to sit. "Henry, I understand you expect me to voluntarily withdraw my name, but I won't. If you give me a direct order, I will not be insubordinate. But before you give the order, I am compelled to say my engineering background fits the needs better than your skills in marketing. So if an AT&T employee is to get the job, the odds are higher for me than you." Henry made no reply, and I went back to call the airlines again. In about an hour Henry came and told me both our names had been submitted. I did not have the heart to tell him I had my airlines reservations and had talked to Julia. She informed me the UN had received Henry's résumé, but I was the one they wanted to interview.

***

A contract for my signature arrived in the mail soon after returning from the interview in Switzerland. My title was to be Chief, Telecommunications Development Unit of the Centre for Telecommunications Development. The ITU wanted the assignment to begin on the first of September. I was scheduled to teach a course in the Bahamas in late September. All arrangements for the course had been finalized. To find a replacement instructor on such short notice was difficult. So I left for Geneva without Shirley in late August with the understanding I would fly to the Bahamas in September to conduct the training. The Bahamas situation gave us an opportunity for a family vacation. Shirley flew from New Jersey, Stephen and Kristi from Texas, and I joined them the weekend before the beginning of the course. It was a fun vacation, but Shirley and Kristi left with both not feeling well.

***

I found an inexpensive hotel within walking distance of my Geneva work location. Everything in Switzerland seemed to be costly. The hotel had about thirty rooms. Most of the other guests were from middle-east countries, and they had short-term visas for service-type work. My small room was on the second floor where I shared a bathroom with other occupants on the floor. Each morning a tray with a cup of hot chocolate, fresh baked bread, butter, and jam was placed outside my door. During the week days, I walked to work. I explored the area around the UN complex on foot after business hours. On weekends, I purchased a public transportation pass which gave access to all buses, trains, and boats for the greater Geneva area. I used the weekends to look for an apartment. The contract with the UN was for one year, but to get the new centre well established would require about five years. Therefore, Shirley and I anticipated being in Switzerland for five years, and finding a comfortable place in a nice location was important. Public transportation was very good, and we were allowed to move one automobile. Therefore, it was not necessary that we reside in Geneva. I found a very nice spacious apartment ten kilometers out of Geneva toward Lausanne. It was the first time I made a living quarters selection without Shirley.

Our apartment was one of five built in a fifteenth-century farm building. The original structure had living quarters for the farm family on one end, and the rest a barn which was large enough for all the livestock during the cold winter months. All five apartments were recently constructed with modern appointments. Shirley's kitchen had granite counter tops with built-in electric range and oven. She also had a clothes drying room, which was very uncommon. The church adjacent to our building was erected in the twelfth century. In it were many weddings and funerals. One funeral of note was for the inventor of Velcro, George de Mestra. Our apartment was unfurnished. The landlord loaned me a bed, table, and two chairs, so I moved from the hotel. The train station in Coppet was just two kilometers from our new address: Route de Founex 2, Commugny, Switzerland. It was a fifteen to twenty minute walk from the train station in Geneva to the UN complex.

***

Back in New Jersey Shirley was not having much luck selling our condo, so we decided to lease it. Shirley was not feeling well while we were in the Bahamas, and

I sensed via our telephone conversations she had gotten worse. I knew Shirley would not want to worry me. Therefore, I talked to Sue Wilson. Sue indicated Shirley was not doing well and recommended I come back as soon as possible.

I was dismayed at the first sight of Shirley when the taxi dropped me off at our Sparta condo. My reaction was for us to head to the emergency room immediately. Shirley was adamant in refusing that option. She, with the help of Sue, had scheduled the movers to pack and load. Shirley and Sue had prepared lists separating items for Switzerland from the ones to be placed in storage. More important Shirley had contacted Dr. Schmid in Chicago, and he had an ex-student, Dr. Georges Fallet, who was a professor in the Department of Rheumatology at the Geneva University Medical School. Dr. Schmid had great confidence in Dr. Fallet and recommended Shirley either come to Chicago or Geneva. Shirley had obtained Dr. Fallet's office and home telephone numbers from Dr. Schmid. Shirley felt, with good reason, that her current doctor in New Jersey was not competent.

"Robert, if you don't get me to either Dr. Fallet or Dr. Schmid soon, I fear I will die."

"Which do you think best?"

"Switzerland, because of your job."

"It is a long flight, are you up to it?"

"I'll have to be."

Chapter 14

Switzerland

It was an airplane flight from hell, but we made it. I rented a car at the Geneva airport, drove Shirley directly to our new home in Commugny, and helped her into bed. Our telephone was connected, so I called Dr. Fallet's office. Not reaching him there, I called his home. He was expecting my call because Dr. Schmid had called him. Dr. Fallet had retired. However, he conveyed to me the name of his replacement, Professor Vischer de Champel. Dr. Vischer had been made aware of Shirley's case by Dr. Fallet. I called Dr. Vischer, and he asked me to read him results from Shirley's most recent blood workup. Some of the information concerned him, particularly the creatinine level. Upon hearing that number, he wanted us to meet him at the hospital as soon as possible. I rushed Shirley to what would be her living accommodations for two of her first three months in Switzerland—L'Hôpital de Beau-Séjour. The last three months of 1987 were not easy. However, early in the year of 1988, Shirley and I knew without a doubt our move to Switzerland had been very beneficial for her health.

***

The assignment in Geneva provided the greatest single advancement of my professional career. The new assignment was roughly equivalent in responsibility, influence, and prestige to an assistant vice president. The beginning UN salary grade (P5-Step 4) afforded me diplomatic privileges (a Pink Card and CD auto plates in Switzerland). I reported directly to Dietrich

Westendoerpf, the head of the centre. Dietrich was from the Federal Republic of Germany (West Germany) and employed by the Deutsche Bundespost prior to his Geneva post. He got the position for which I had applied during the Puerto Rico years. The deputy to Dietrich was a Tunisian named Ahmed Laouyane. Both reported to Richard Butler, ITU Secretary-General. Mr. Butler's nationality was Australian.

My peer, Saturo Hashimoto, Chief of the Operations Support Unit, was from Japan. Saturo and I had a good rapport. He was a pleasure in the office and a delightful golf companion. Because of political considerations, the third unit head was not filled. A Soviet citizen, Leonid Androuchko, was hired and the duties scaled back to a lower salary grade. Leonid had been the director of the telephone institute in Kiev. He was a Soviet, but made it clear he was Ukrainian not Russian. Leonid and his family were friends of Shirley and me. After Shirley and I retired, I did some contract work and was a guest in the Androuchko's apartment while in Geneva to write final reports.

***

An interesting and informative event happened about six months into the UN assignment. Shirley and I were very much on a learning curve. She knew the French words for useful foods, and had fallen in love with the fresh produce in local farmer's markets. Going to the bakery in Coppet where there was a large array of freshly baked items was always enjoyable for her. An English-speaking church in Geneva had a library from which she could check out books, and once a week or so, we rented an English speaking video. My French language skills were not up to a novice level yet, but they surpassed my comprehension of diplomatic protocols. AT&T top level executives had arranged for a formal meeting with Mr. Butler, Secretary-General of the ITU. I was on the cusp of exposure to this type of high level negotiations. The top three AT&T executives were coming. They were: James Olson, AT&T Chairman; Robert Allen, AT&T President; and John Hinds, AT&T International President.

Dietrich explained the process. The Secretary-General met alone with the visiting delegation. Mr. Westendoerpf was then summoned to Mr. Butler's office. As he left, Dietrich told me to stay near my telephone. After about an hour, Mr. Butler's secretary called and said, "The Secretary-General requests you to come to his office to greet your counterpart, Mr. John Hinds, and the rest of the AT&T delegation." It was strange to be referred to as an equal of Mr. Hinds, but I liked the idea. Mr. Butler's office was befitting of his position, and I would have been intimidated if it had been my first time to enter. Mr. Olson stood up and came to greet me. I knew an AT&T staff person had done a good job when Mr. Olson shook my hand and said, "Robert, how are you doing? Are you and Shirley enjoying Switzerland?" I replied as if we actually knew each other. Mr. Olson then turned to Mr. Butler and inquired, "Are you pleased with Robert's job performance?" Mr. Butler said nice things about me, and Dietrich reinforced Mr. Butler's positive evaluation. Mr. Hinds then addressed me saying in a joking tone, "Well, Robert, guess you have not had time to screw up yet."

***

Our group was created with one characteristic not common in most multilateral assistance programs. The resources, money and in-kind, for our in-country development projects were not part of the ITU's regular budget. Our administrative costs were paid from budgeted funds, but we had to find willing donors (governments, other multilateral organizations, NGOs, corporations, foundations, etc.) to cover the capital, personnel, equipment, and supplies needed on a project-by-project basis. This allowed us to select the person with project oversight responsibility. In other words, we would not send resources directly to a country to be used as the local officials saw fit. Our chosen supervisor was to be from the outside and most would come from a developed country. My job was to review requests for assistance from developing countries, and then define the scope and details for implementation. Formal documents of exact details were prepared by me, and then approved by the requesting country. Missions to the country were often required for me to understand the request or more often to explain the details.

***

I knew we had a problem as soon as our over-loaded small taxi pulled up to the entrance of our hotel in Bangkok, Thailand. Shirley and I were in the back seat with two suitcases—one between us and one in my lap. Leonid Androuchko was in the passenger-side front seat holding a small bag. The rest of Leonid's and our luggage was crammed into the car's tiny trunk. The three of us were scheduled to be in Bangkok for two weeks. Leonid and I were to attend a regional telecommunications conference, and Shirley would have a vacation. After the close of the conference Shirley and Leonid were to fly back to Geneva, and I would travel on to Sri Lanka and Pakistan.

Leonid had volunteered to make the hotel reservations. He had a purpose. Our per diem was $90.

Like many other UN employees from developing countries, Leonid knew how to return home with money in his pocket—find a hotel for less than $30 with free breakfast; skip lunch and go heavy on the snacks at the morning and afternoon breaks; and pig-out on happy hour hors d'oeuvres provided by the telephone equipment manufacturers.

A cheap hotel in a seedy section of Bangkok in 1989 was not an inviting place to spend two weeks. Shirley and I did not check into our reserved room. I started calling hotels. All of the name-brand hotels were booked. I broke a rule, and called the AT&T country manager. He and I had worked together in New Jersey. When told of our situation, he said he would make some calls and get back with me. He called back in about thirty minutes with bad news. We would have to stay where we were for one night, and he would have his secretary find us a more suitable place the next morning. Needless to say it was not a restful night of sleep. The secretary called Shirley before noon the next day and told her to take a cab to the Bangkok Hilton. She gave Shirley one caveat: the Hilton's staff might have an impression Shirley was the wife of an AT&T vice president. The rate was $110 per night, and Shirley said it was worth every penny. She slept in every day. The hotel had fine restaurants, and each afternoon a driver in a white Mercedes took her to points of interest in Bangkok.

The conference's last meeting was on Friday morning March 10. Shirley had flight reservations to depart for Geneva on Saturday the eleventh, and mine was for the same day headed to Sri Lanka. The man who headed the network planning group in Thailand approached me and requested a meeting for Friday afternoon. He and I discussed planning and economic evaluation issues for two hours in his office. As we were about to say our good byes, I noticed a golf trophy in his book shelf. After he determined I also played, he invited me to join his normal Saturday group. When advised of Shirley's and my flight plans, he said, "Don't worry, my secretary will change your flight and arrange for a driver to take your wife to the airport."

The course we played was used mostly by the Thais. We were a six-some. Five to eight per group was common. I knew no one in the group except the man who invited me. There were two good golfers in the group, and others were about my speed. I knew nothing of their skill levels, nor did they of mine. We each had a caddy, and one of the better golfers had two—one for his bag and another for his umbrella and portable stool. All the caddies were females except one. Mine was a young woman who stood about four feet and ten inches. She knew maybe fifty words in English (par, pin, green, one, two...), and one two-word expression—"Oh, no!" My caddy did all she could to help me. All the caddies knew the course very well—especially, how to read the greens.

We went to the first hole—all thirteen of us. In one group I counted twenty-seven people. You would have thought it a tournament rather than regular play. The first hole was a dog-leg to the left of 385 yards, if you played the fairway. There was a large pond on the left in the dog-leg. Thus, for a good golfer there were two alternatives—play a long iron off the tee and a second shot of 120 yards over the pond, or hit a wood past the pond and have a second shot of 150 yards and no water. Since I could not drive past the pond, my plan was to play my normal tee shot of 180 yards, then use a four-wood over the right edge of the pond leaving me a twenty-yard chip and two putts for a bogie.

Being a guest, I hit first. Much to my surprise my ball did not fade and if I were not a short hitter would have been in the pond. My ball ended up four yards from the water and 130 yards from the edge of the green. At least 120 yards of the distance was liquid—not where I wanted to be. But since a good golfer might play the hole that way, I put on my confident face and walked from the tee as if I had hit my desired shot.

When we reached my ball my caddy tried to give me a seven-iron. I didn't know what was behind the green, but I sure could see the trouble in front. I insisted on a five-iron over the strong objections of my caddy. She finally gave me the five. I struck it dead on the pin landing five feet short of the hole. My ball rolled within a few inches of the cup and about six feet past. From there I had a difficult down-hill putt for a birdie. I stroked it smooth in to the heart of the hole. Walking off the green, I added a swagger to my step while my caddy reported to all within shouting range something in Thai ending with the word *birdie*.

The second hole was a nice, wide and straight par four. Teeing off in my earned first position, my drive was down the middle. I had them worried, and the first hole had been so great, I temporally felt as if they had reason. The fact I make a birdie only once in every ten rounds was forgotten. I was sure to leave the second green one or two under. When I asked for a four-iron for my second, my caddy handed it to me with a smile on her face that said, *it's good to caddy for a golfer who knows his game.* Jack Nicklaus would have been proud to hit a four-iron the way I did. As soon as the club face made contact with the ball, I heard my caddy use her "Oh no!" expression the first of many times. Needless to say the ball was just getting up to speed as it passed above the flag—it was directly on line. Three shots later, I finally found the green and with four putts scored a nine.

***

Bad break #1:

My first night in Karachi was not routine. First, my flight was delayed, and my plane did not touch down until very late in the evening. During UN orientation it was advised to schedule air transportation for arrival times before noon on any mission to a country in a state of unrest. Pakistan fit that profile.

Bad break #2:

There had been a miscommunication with the UN office in Karachi. I anticipated a representative to meet me in the baggage claim area. The envoy was not there.

Bad break #3:

I found a public telephone in the secure luggage area and dialed the UN office number. The office was closed.

Bad break #4:

I had spent nights in airports before. Thus, staying where I was seemed like a good idea. I found a corner for my suit bag, suitcase, and me. The UN office would be open in the morning to receive my call. Soon the last arrival of the night had landed and all passengers had collected their gear, and luggage handlers began to close-up. A security officer approached me. My sad story and UN Laissez-Passer did not persuade him. I was escorted to a door into the section containing the airline check-in counters.

Bad break #5:

Maybe this part of the airport would remain open all night? So I asked a security person near a ticket counter, "Is it permitted for me to stay here?"

"No," said the guard. "Sir, you get a taxi to take you to your hotel."

I explained I did not know the name of the hotel

because the reservations had been made by the UN office.

"The taxi driver knows of hotels nearby. You must leave the terminal."

Bad break #6:

There were no cars in the taxi stand. In fact there were no other people or vehicles. I stood wondering what to do but not for long. The guard came out and pointed to the entrance gate in the high security fence on the outer perimeter of the airport and said, "Sir, the taxis are outside the gate. You must go there."

I walked toward the airport entrance gate, but I had absolutely no intention of venturing into the unknown beyond the security fence. The gate was about one hundred meters from me. There were outside lights on the terminal and in the area of the entrance gate. It was a dark night, and there was an unlighted area between the building and gate. I did not glance back until I was in the dark spot. The guard had returned into the building.

Good break #1:

I ran back toward the building, but not to the door of my exit. Once at the building I stood quietly with my back tightly against the outside wall. I stayed in that position long enough to catch my breath and be convinced neither the guard, nor anyone else knew I was there.

Good break #2:

Creeping along the outside of the structure in the direction away from the guard, I found a small alcove.

Good break #3:

Located in the alcove was a portable money-exchange kiosk. There were about two meters of space on each side—plenty of room for me and my bags.

There I stayed undisturbed for the rest of the night. Awakened by the early morning airport bustle, I went inside the terminal, found a restroom, freshened up a bit, and called the UN office.

***

The new smaller, deregulated AT&T necessitated a reduced workforce. In the fall of 1989 an early retirement incentive package was offered. I had vested rights even though not on their payroll. Thus, Shirley and I qualified.

If we agreed to the offer, then we would start receiving a pension check in January of 1990. Our contract with the UN ran until the end of December of 1990, and renewal for at least two more years was assured. Staying until the end of ninety-two would have given me five years of UN service, and qualified us for a generous international service pension. I liked the job and wanted to stay. An AT&T pension plus the UN salary would have been nice. At first, Shirley agreed. However, she later changed her mind.

"Robert, both our mothers are getting older, and I also want to be there when our first grandchild is born. I want to go home."

Therefore, I requested an early release from my UN contract. We moved back to Texas in the summer of 1990. During December of 1989 the following notice was circulated in the Basking Ridge headquarters of AT&T International:

ORGANIZATION NOTICE
AT&T International
Robert H. Baldwin, currently on

loan from AT&T International to the International Telecommunications Union (ITU) in Geneva, Switzerland will retire on December 30, 1989 after more than 22 years of service.

Before relocating to Switzerland, Robert was responsible for the AT&T International staff results function in Basking Ridge, New Jersey. Prior to that, he was on assignment in Puerto Rico with the AT&T International Advisory Services organization working with the Puerto Rico Telephone Company.

I am sure you will join me in wishing Robert well in all his future endeavors.

W.K. Lindhorst
International Public Affairs,
Policy and Administration
Vice President

We stopped over in New Jersey on the way to Texas to take care of some loose ends. While there, Mr. Hinds wanted me to drop by his office. We talked for more than two hours. Mr. Hinds asked detailed questions about the UN, my assignment, and the state of international networks. As he walked me to his office door he said, "Robert, I am told you think I have a poor opinion of you. That is not true. From the beginning, I was impressed with your job performance." I was tempted but did not say, "*Follow me to the conference room on the second floor, and let's see if my blood-stains in the southwest corner of that room are still visible.*"

Our apartment in Commugny

Dietrich Westendoerpf, Saturo Hashimoto, me

My hotel before Shirley joined me

Chapter 15

Bon Coïncidence

Shirley's and my years of exposure to the world stage occurred simultaneously with a seismic change in the world's experiment with Communism. The time frame was between early autumn of 1987 and late fall of 1990. It included our Switzerland years plus the first few months of retirement in Kerrville. During that period, the Soviet Union imploded. The economics of China and Vietnam transformed from centrally planned into market economies. Cuba treaded water, and the hermit kingdom of North Korea sank deeper into deprivation and isolation. A historian, political scientist, or economist might have been better able to understand and put into context the things I heard and observed back then. But even I, a mere telephone man, knew it was a significant world historical moment.

***

I did not become a dedicated advocate of privatization of government-owned telecoms until after having a long dinner with one of the architects of the AT&T divestiture. He was a government employee. My meeting with him was in a restaurant in Geneva after my appointment to the UN assignment.

My Puerto Rico assignment was serendipitous, but not nearly the scale of the one with the UN. There my status gave me influence and opportunities not possible within the structure of the Bell System. There was only one level of management between the Secretary General and me. I headed all my mission trips. In-country counterparts were vice-ministers, and they were facing major network changes in the late 1980s. In most communist countries the telecom

137

adjustments were handled simultaneously with the collapse of their political system. The environment was ripe for an interesting work assignment. It was a fascinating challenge to sow the seeds of a market-based provision of telecommunications services in countries with weak, centrally-planned economies. It was an experience far beyond the wildest fantasies of an eight-year-old cotton boll-puller from the South Plains of Texas.

***

It happened during the first break of my first meeting with telephone people from member countries of the ITU. Lars Engvall, a Swedish co-worker, took me aside and asked, "When are you going to say something?"

"Being new, I think it best to just listen."

"Don't you understand?"

"Understand what?"

"You are the highest ranking official from the United States, and nothing of substance will get done until the obligatory Cold War ritual."

"Huh?"

"All you need to do is find an inconsequential item and state your opinion. The Soviet delegate will then, being very diplomatic, slightly disagree with you on some minor point. Someone from the West will then stand in support of you." Lars teased," I might do it, if your observation is accidentally profound." He continued, "After a couple more East-West exchanges, the meeting will move to actually addressing the telecommunication issue." I am happy to report once telephone people got past politics, we spoke the same language.

***

138

Mid-way into my UN assignment, there was a conference in Geneva of the heads of telecommunication research and development organizations in their respective countries. The envoy from Bulgaria was a relatively young intellectual, and a very personable man. He was staying in Geneva a few days at the close of the forum and requested a private consultation. After talk about our backgrounds, he shifted to a delicate, confidential matter. Utilizing carefully chosen words (he was a master of his second language, English) he implied that he did not subscribe to the political ideology of Marx and Lenin.

"Why are you telling me this?"

"Because I do not want you to think I am a fool."

He went on to say that almost all of his peers held the same view. But they had to be judicious where and with whom to speak the truth. According to him, the largest cadre of true believers was on the university campuses in the West.

***

In November of 1988 I traveled with Mr. Marcel Scoffier for a seventeen-day mission to the People's Republic of China (PRC). Mr. Scoffier was a Frenchman with a long career as an employee of The World Bank. Our objective was to define the details of a possible project for development of rural telecommunications in the Shandong Province of China.

After meeting with officials in Beijing (details of that time will be discussed later in the chapter), we took an Air China flight to Jinan, the capital of the Shandong Province. From Jinan, the Chinese provincial telephone officials escorted us on a mini-bus for a seven-day field visit of nearly 2000 kilometers. Our party consisted of about ten people. Our primary destination was Weihai City which is on the Yellow Sea at the eastern tip of the Shandong Province. On the route to Weihai City, we stayed in hotels in Weifang and Yantal. On the return

139

trip, Qingdao was an overnight stop. Mr. Scoffier and I held meetings and classes for telephone personnel at many locations. I discussed how to plan a telephone development project, and Mr. Scoffier explained the international process for obtaining funds required for implementation.

The stops each night were most interesting. Our hotels were the best (and sometimes the only) one in town. There was a formal meeting and dinner with local government officials, usually the mayor and some of his deputies. The proceedings began with the mayor and me seated in stuffed chairs with doilies on each armrest, a small table between us, with interpreters standing behind us. There would be toasts and pictures taken. After dinner Mr. Scoffier and I would rush to our rooms to draw bath water as there was hot water for only two hours each day. I used the water in one of the two thermoses placed outside my door each morning to shave. Heat was not turned on in any location except Beijing until November 15. Thus, I wore sweaters and a top coat at all times and jumped into the warmth of my bed with two heavy wool blankets immediately after bathing.

The scope of commercial activities taking place along our route was astonishing. Mr. Scoffier indicated he had not seen anything similar in other developing countries; his travels with The World Bank had taken him into many. Family-type operations were common with each family in an area working separately but producing the same output. There was little mechanization even on the larger scale activities. We were taken to one very large granite quarry, the scope of which was comparable to an open-pit coal mine in Wyoming. There were tens of thousands of Chinese using only hammers and chisels to excavate construction-size granite blocks. The blocks were carried by hand from the quarry floor and loaded on ox pulled or human pushed carts.

Our last night in Jinan afforded a unique opportunity to have a brief glimpse into the thinking of a young Chinese professional. The last formal dinner had ended, and all the high ranking officials had left the hotel. Mr. Scoffier had gone to his room leaving me with our interpreter and a young engineer from the telephone office in Jinan. This engineer had been assigned to assist Mr. Scoffier and me during our time in the province. Thus, he and I had much contact. He spoke little English and no Spanish or French; therefore, our verbal communications were with the aid of our interpreter.

With just the three of us in the hotel lobby, the young engineer wanted to finally have time to ask me personal questions. I wisely agreed to miss my hot bath for the chance for an informal visit. We talked until almost daylight. He had never seen a person from the West, much less traveled and talked with one. We learned much about each other. Though different in age by twenty years, he saw some similarities in the thirty years of his life and the first three decades of mine. Both of us were college graduates, telephone company engineers, and married with one child. He zeroed in on our differences: I owned a three-bedroom and two-bath house, he lived in a small apartment with his wife's parents; I had two automobiles, he had none and little hope of one in the future. His last question was a good one, "We Chinese have a longer cultural history, are as smart, work as hard, and have the same desires as you Americans. All of that being true why did you, at age thirty, have much more of life's conveniences than I now have?"

***

I almost did not allow the trip to the Shandong Province to happen. When Mr. Scoffier and I first arrived in Beijing, there was a substantive meeting with officials from the Ministry of Posts and Telecommunications (MPTC). Mr. Liu Zhongen, Deputy Director of the Department of External Affairs led the Chinese delegation. The meeting was in the evening after a formal welcoming dinner. Things turned a little tense soon after the opening pleasantries. There was an agreement concerning the scope and objective of our fact-finding trip to the province, but Mr. Zhongen made it very clear that the resulting developmental project must conform to their desires. First and foremost, there was not to be a person selected by the UN to oversee the project. They wanted money and equipment and nothing more. I advised him of the centre's policy. Without our person working with Chinese personnel, we would not be involved. He assured me of the capabilities of the telephone engineers in the Shandong Province. I told him that was not the issue. It was clear we were not going to be able to arrive at a compromise.

I told Mr. Zhongen, "A trip to the province would be a waste of everyone's time. Please, have your personnel arrange a flight for Mr. Scoffier back to New York and me to Geneva."

I thanked him for the fine meal and the frank discussion, and excused myself. Mr. Scoffier followed me out, and when we were out of earshot, he said, "Robert, you can't do this."

"I just did."

"But no UN person submits a report saying his mission was a failure."

"My report will state my view of the facts."

I went to my hotel room and Mr. Scoffier to his. In about an hour there was a knock on my door. It was the interpreter, and Mr. Zhongen had sent him to explain the situation. All the arrangements for our trip to the province had been made. No one from the West had ever been to the scheduled locations. To have a Frenchman from the World Bank and a US citizen with the UN was a very big deal for local officials. It would be very embarrassing if we did not show. The proposal was for Mr. Scoffier and me to make the trip, but there would be no follow-up project. I expressed regret for the awkward position for the local officials. But since the original objective had disappeared, I could not justify a long and costly trip with the sole purpose of relieving an uncomfortable situation. The young man left, and I went to bed.

It was not long until the interpreter woke me. This time he had been instructed to be very forthright and brutally frank. If Mr. Scoffier and I did not go, the consequences were not a question of mere embarrassment. At a minimum, careers would be destroyed, and for some it could be a matter of life or death. *Whoa! Can it be true?* The interpreter's eyes and voice tone convinced me not to risk that he was overly dramatic. I awakened Mr. Scoffier and told him of the events since we last parted. We would go, but we would also do something useful. I could teach some highlights from a course on network development and economic decision-making, while he could complement my efforts with his knowledge of international finance and procurement procedures. Mr. Scoffier liked the idea. We sketched out the details and summoned the interpreter. All agreed. In cold classrooms across the Shandong Province, Mr. Scoffier and I shared our knowledge with eager Chinese telephone engineers. It seemed to be a rewarding experience for all involved.

***

My name was added to a short list when my right foot touched the tarmac of the North Korean Pyongyang Sunan International Airport at 10:35am on April 19, 1990. The Korean conflict ended in July of 1953. The already-tight borders of the Democratic People's Republic of Korea (DPRK), better known as North Korea, closed even more and especially for US citizens. To say North Korea was careful with visas issued to US citizens would be an understatement. The North's distaste for Americans may have been greater than for fellow Koreans south of the thirty-eighth parallel.

DPRK issued few entry visas between 1953 and 1990 to people with US passports. All issued before 1972 were to avowed communists and others sympathetic to Kim Il-sung. President Nixon's trip to China in February of 1972 was a catalyst which opened North Korea to a limited number of non-communists US citizens. Visas issued between 1972 and 1990 can be placed into three categories. There were those which North Korea allowed to enter for strategic political reasons. This category included three US journalists in 1972, US Congressman Stephen Solarz in 1980, three people from the American Friends Service Committee also in 1980, and about 15 American scholars of Korea in 1981. The second category was US citizens attending international events staged in Pyongyang. There were two of these. In 1979 North Korea hosted the 35th World Table Tennis Championships. In response to the 1988 Summer Olympics in Seoul, South Korea, North Korea was awarded the 13th World Festival of Students and Youth in 1989. The third category was people for which the DPRK did not want to issue a visa and only did so after outside political pressure. I was in this group. There were only two others. Professor Jerome A. Cohen obtained a DPRK visa (which included his family) in 1972. Dr. Cohen was a Professor of Law at New York University with expertise in China's legal system. He had contacts in China who helped arrange his trip. Peter Hyun was born and reared in the north of Korea. He left Korea in 1948 and later gained his US citizenship. It took him three years of effort with the DPRK embassies in Havana and Algiers to obtain his visa. Peter spent three weeks in North Korea in 1979. The North Korean government did not want to issue my visa, but my general secretariat held firm. I entered using my UN Laissez-Passer. Being third of three in this category doesn't make me unique, but it comes close. Certainly, I was there before Billy Graham (1992) and ex-President Carter (1994).

Even with a visa, flying from Geneva to Pyongyang was a logistical nightmare. Mr. Eberhard Roegner, an outside plant expert from West Germany, traveled with me. I met him at the Sheremetyevo International Airport located northwest of Moscow. A car with driver from the ministry transported us to the Domodedovo Airport which was an hour's ride to the southeast of Moscow. Our driver pulled up to the main entrance of the dreary two-level terminal. There was a line of people snaking outside the door. They had wrapped their suitcases in white butcher-type paper which was secured with rope. I found out later this was to deter theft by the baggage handlers. Our driver escorted us into the terminal past the glaring eyes of the members of the queue.

The check-in counter lobby was packed. The driver transferred us into the care of a uniformed airport official who told us to follow closely. The officer muscled a path thorough the mass of passengers to stairs to the second level. The large waiting area on level-two was devoid of any travelers except Eberhard and me. We were in the part of the building reserved for people holding tickets purchased with hard currency. The throng of people in the lobby below us were Soviets who could fly Aeroflot domestic flights for about thirty rubles (less than twenty dollars). Eberhard and I showed the woman at the counter our tickets. She recorded our names on a yellow pad. I asked about boarding passes, and she indicated they were not needed as we were the only two passengers who would board from our gate. Eberhard and I watched from the second level window as the Soviets walked across the tarmac and up the steps into the airplane. It took a while, but finally we were the only two left to board a full flight. We had our own private bus to get from terminal to airplane. There was no one on the plane who spoke English, German, Spanish, or French. It was going to be an interesting thirteen hours before we landed at Khabarovsk's Novy Airport.

There were six seats per row—three on each side. Two across-the-aisle seats near mid-plane were held for Eberhard and me. There was a commotion in our area by the time we were seated. Next to Eberhard was a mother in the middle seat with her son at the window. The father and another son were in the aisle and middle seats in the row in front of me. The boy in the row in front of me was very upset that his brother had a window, and he did not. When I say the boy was upset, I mean he was having a screaming fit. There were women in the middle and window seats next to me. I had what seemed to be a good idea at the time. If I could make the woman next to me understand, and she agreed we would move up one row, and maybe the father and his son being on the same row with the mother and other son would calm the situation. The woman next to me and the father seemed to comprehend my pointing and gesturing, and they liked the idea. The boy stopped crying, and for a brief period I was a hero as the people in our area cheered. When we started changing seats I realized there was a problem. The woman next to me grabbed the aisle seat vacated by the father. I thought— *oh well, having the adulation negated the inconvenience of middle versus aisle seat.* The father either thought the woman at the window was also part of the bargain, or he tried to convince her to let his son have her window seat. "Het!" was her response. The boy started to cry again. The woman at the window became a pariah. There were boos. Eberhard had the solution. He would give up his seat to the boy. I was to sit in the middle seat next to the *het* woman, and Eberhard would be directly in front of me. Thirteen hours seated by a woman who was hated by her fellow passengers because of me, was not the sort of flight I had in mind. With time her scowl dissipated, and she later noted a skyline picture of New York City in an old *Life* magazine which was given to me by the flight attendant. I guessed she wanted to know if I was from New York. I said, "Het, Texas."

Her eyes lit up as she nearly shouted, "Dallas." Her reaction was common in many places where I traveled in the late nineteen eighties. I think the entire world had access to that popular television show. The remainder of the thirteen hours to Khabarovsk was not so difficult. I even got some sleep. After a short night in Khabarovsk, an international Aeroflot flight ferried us to North Korea.

Nice looking young females in blue uniforms immediately caught my eye upon entry into Pyongyang. There was one of these women at most street intersections. Their job, I suppose, was to direct almost nonexistent vehicular traffic. Each one did give us a big smile and wave. That was a common reaction to all who spotted the black Lada in which we were riding. Eberhard and I were taken directly to the Koryo Hotel, a modern twin-tower high-rise structure. The quantity of people in the lobby seemed normal for a downtown hotel during an early Thursday afternoon, but the mood was subdued. Most were talking quietly in small groups— some standing and others seated on inexpensive, Scandinavian looking furniture. It was an eclectic mixture of folks. There were a few from the West— France and West Germany mostly. Wearing pants that fit no one, held up by a one-size-for-all belt, identified men from East European countries. Even Communism could not take away the Caribbean style of the Cubans. North Koreans were easy to spot by the ubiquitous lapel pins with a picture of the *great leader*, except for the young men in dark-colored, tight-fitting suits. Four or five of them were always in the lobby—moving about or pretending to read a newspaper. They did not wear Kim Il-sung picture pins.

Eberhard and I each had an interpreter. We were never in the company of a single North Korean since there were always two or more when in our presence. Our interpreters were not allowed to see their families during our stay. In theory we were free to explore the city, and we did see a lot. When we walked the city streets, we were always followed; and subtlety was not a characteristic of those assigned the task. Our *shadows* never directly interfered with our movements. Once Eberhard and I were denied entrance into what appeared to be an indoor farmers' produce market. However, a guard at the door stopped us, not the *tail* behind us.

I have a special memory associated with one of our walking tours. As we passed a North Korean version of a department store, I spotted a toy airplane constructed of tin. It had a wing span of about eighteen inches. I had not seen a toy made of tin in years.

"Eberhard, let's go in, I want to buy that toy."

All inside spoke only Korean. Nonetheless, the female clerk understood my desire to purchase the airplane. I had previously changed Swiss francs into North Korean wons at the hotel. When I placed the North Korean currency on the counter, the clerk jumped back, wide-eyed with fear. She made no sound while her eyes were frantically changing focus from the money on the counter to the two guards approaching me. Each guard had an AK47 gripped firmly against his chest at forty-five degrees off perpendicular. No one said a word. Calmly and slowly I retrieved the bills and turned and accompanied Eberhard out the door. We later learned there were two types of won. A local is not allowed to possess any hard-currency wons. Also, the next morning at the start of our meeting I was asked if I wanted to go shopping—perhaps for toys. I hoped I would buy the airplane. Wrong. They took us to a hard-currency store on the edge of the city, which had only cheap plastic toys made in China.

Please don't get the wrong impression. Eberhard and I did more than just play tourist. Real telephone work was done. It was done mostly by Eberhard after I returned to Geneva. My role was to negotiate the terms. The North Koreans were like many other officials from a developing country. They just wanted funds and equipment provided without UN oversight. But they were more persistent than most. The first meeting on the day of arrival was with Mr. Jang Bong-jin, Vice Minister. I tried to explain our policy very clearly to the vice minister in hopes we could proceed without further hassle. The same issue was discussed repeatedly. By the end of the North Korean mission, I had been with the UN for three years and had learned how to remain diplomatically firm.

***

In November of 1989 people with access to live television watched the breaching of the Berlin Wall. Young Germans with small hand tools gave the world a picture of the realities in the Soviet Empire. The dictatorial system which had taken seven decades to create was being quickly dismantled by its inhabitants.

In 1922 Ukraine became a founding member of the Union of Soviet Socialist Republics (USSR). The Ukrainians did not obtain complete separation until the final collapse of the USSR in late 1991. However, the telephone administrators in Kiev foresaw the need to begin preparations to operate their network without control from Moscow. In late 1990 with the help of Leonid Androuchko the UN agreed to provide Ukraine with Western telecommunications techniques. By this time Shirley and I were living in Kerrville. Mr. Westendoerpf contacted me to head the mission. I arranged for Al Loya to accompany me. Al was owner of EduTech, Inc. based in Denver, Colorado. He and I had worked together on the development of telecommunication training materials. In Kiev, Al and I taught a five day seminar. It was an advantageous time and place to view a small slice of history in the making.

Al, our interpreter, and I were walking down the hallway of a telephone building in Kiev when we came upon a bust of Lenin which had not yet been removed. On the pedestal for the bust was an inscription. I asked the interpreter for a translation. He read it and then gave us a paraphrase: "It says, 'the destiny of USSR citizens is to spread the beneficial fruits of Communism to all of humanity'." The young man turned to Al and me and said, "It did not happen, did it?"

Another event of note occurred after completion of the seminar, just prior to Al's and my departure. Our interpreter and the young man who had been assigned as Al's and my escort wanted us to go to one of their apartments and meet their spouses. We jumped at the chance. An opportunity like this would not have been possible just a few months earlier. We would have to spend the night because of the inadequacy of local transportation. The apartment was on a high floor of a drab concrete building like so many more in all USSR cities. We climbed the stairs as the elevators did not work. The stairwell was poorly lit with lots of litter. The apartment was small, probably less than a thousand square feet. It was the living quarters for the young couple, their toddler son, and the wife's parents. The older couple and the young boy were asleep due to the late hour of our arrival. Cheese and chocolate candy were on the coffee table for snacks for the six of us (the two young couples, Al, and me).

The two women had never met anyone from the West. They had numerous questions. Both were professionals. One was a professor of Russian literature at a university, and I do not remember the other's occupation. The agreement was if Al and I answered their questions, then they would respond to our inquiries. I asked them to tell the details of a typical week in their lives. The answers were eye-opening. Just standing in lines to obtain the staples of life was a full time effort—not counting being a mother, wife, and holding down a job. I wanted to know how they did it. The professor admitted it was a grind, but she stayed upbeat by concentrating on the good things in her life: a good husband, a healthy son, family, and friends. I then asked what may have been an impolite question. "What about your son? Do you desire him to have your life?"

Tears rolled down her cheeks as her husband emotionally answered for them both, "No, no, never— our son must have better!"

***

My trip home was via Geneva where I wrote the report of the mission. Leonid invited me to stay in his apartment. He had been able to bring his and his wife's parents to Geneva. With the unrest taking place in Ukraine, Geneva was a safe haven. The apartment was spacious but with six adults and a teenage son, it was full. I volunteered to get a hotel room. Leonid insisted I spend the night with him and his extended family. I am glad I did. He and I talked late into the night. He wanted details of the mission to Kiev. When I relayed the story about the bust of Lenin, I spoke in a less than serious tone. I could tell he was bothered.

"What's wrong, Leonid?"

"Robert, there are four people asleep in that bedroom who spent their lives believing the words of Lenin. Now, in their seventies they learn it was all lies. My heart breaks for them."

Boys at an arcade game in North Korea in 1990

Mini-bus group in China

Chapter 16

Kerrville

Shirley's quality of life in Switzerland was relatively good—with the exception of the first three months. However, Dr. Vischer had advised us of adjustments we would soon be making. The function of one of her kidneys was below ten percent, and the other was not perfect. Two options were available: dialysis or a kidney transplant. If we had remained in Switzerland, dialysis would have been the sole alternative.

Once back in the states, we purchased a lot in Kerrville and signed a contract with Ron Coryell to construct the house of our dreams. We moved in April of 1991. I completed my last contract as a telecommunications consultant in October of that year. Dr. Claudia Hura, a nephrologist in San Antonio became Shirley's primary doctor.

***

After Daddy's death Mother had moved from the parsonage in Frio to a small two-bedroom, one-bath house in Hereford. It was not easy for her, but she made the necessary adjustments, and in time she built a rewarding life for herself. She supplemented the small pension from Daddy's years of teaching by opening a daycare operation in her home. She did this for many years. Near the end, offspring of her earlier children were in Mother's care. Mother started a family tradition, a form of which exists today. During the Christmas holidays, she hosted a family get-together. She selected a theme and wrote a program script. The highlight was a performance by her grandchildren. Mother authored an account of her life from birth until Daddy's death.

Mother's health began to decline soon after her eightieth birthday and became much worse while Shirley and I were in Switzerland. It was bad enough to necessitate a move to Dallas. There she lived in an apartment complex near my sister Mary. Wynelle and Eugene were also in the area. It was there I visited her during the first months after my retirement. Mother and I had good visits. I thank God Shirley convinced me not to stay in Switzerland for two more years. As Mother's health declined, she regressed though all the stages: independent living, assisted living, and skilled nursing care. Her emotional state declined with each loss of independence. With Mother's natural upbeat personality, it was difficult for me to detect periods of melancholy. She understood the unpleasantness of being around someone with a grumpy attitude. Thus, Mother made sure she was pleasant.

Shirley and I were celebrating Thanksgiving with Shirley's mother Annie in Hereford when the call came. Wynelle indicated Mother was being transported from the eldercare home in Denton to the hospital, and the situation did not look hopeful. Eugene and Bonnie were also in Hereford for the holiday. The three of us (Eugene, Bonnie, and I) flew from Amarillo to Dallas. The doctor wanted Mother to agree to gallbladder surgery. The doctor's rationale was vague. Mother had never had surgery and did not desire any so late in life. She turned the final decision over to her children. After prayerful consideration we decided surgery was not in Mother's best interest. She seemed relieved. A schedule was set for at least one of us to be with Mother at all times, and my period was during daylight hours. Mother was most alert early in the mornings; her mental faculties were still strong for a person of eighty-eight. When all the family was in her room, she liked for us to pray and sing hymns. There were tears mixed with remembrances of happy and difficult periods. Once after a very emotional phase, I decided to lighten the atmosphere by saying,

"Mother, I think this would be a great opportunity for you to tell all my brothers and sisters that I am your favorite."

Her response was vintage Blanche Keene Baldwin.

"Yes, Robert, if I *were* going to say I liked you best, this would be the perfect moment to express it."

Mother and I did have intervals alone. Kristi was pregnant with a due date in early January. I had a sonogram with a bean-shaped image. Thus, with Stephen and Kristi's fondness for nicknames, they referred to Shirley's and my future grandchild as *Beanie*. Mother and I would talk about *Beanie*. We both marveled at the coincidence of Kristi's birth soon after Daddy's death, and *Beanie's* birth soon after her pending death. At one point Mother said, "Robert, please tell *Beanie* about me." I hope this book helps fulfill Mother's request, not just for *Beanie* but also for all other descendants.

Ben Dean, Mary's husband, had cancer and was not doing well. Therefore, scheduling Mary to be with Mother was a real issue. On the night of November 30, I stayed later than normal. It turned out to be a horrific experience. Mother's vital organs started to shut down, and she began to drown in her own body fluids. Watching this happen to anyone is awful beyond words and more so if the person is a loved one. Olagene and her husband, Richard Crum, were doing all they could to comfort Mother. I was at a total loss of what to do. Reflexively I called Mary, and she indicated she would come immediately. Back in the room I joined Ola and Richard in our vain efforts to relieve Mother's anguish. Wesley Earp, Wynelle's husband, was also there helping. Realizing the end was near, Wes left to get Wynelle. Upon Mary's arrival, I inappropriately left the hospital. When I got about half-way across the parking lot, it finally hit me that I must return. While I was out of the room, Mary and Ola had implored the nurse to do something for Mother, and by the time I returned, the heavy dose of Valium had started to work. Mother was calm, and she gave me a smile of recognition and reassurance. In a very short period she was gone to be eternally with Daddy.

***

Cale Robert Williams arrived on January 6, 1993, and Shirley and I became grandparents. From the beginning, we knew it was great—someone to love and spoil rotten while leaving the difficult issues to the parents. We took credit for the positive and shifted the blame to in-laws for those less desirable issues. Not that our grandson ever possessed many of the undesirable ones. To have one grandchild is awesome, and yet the second more than doubles the pleasures. This event happened on December 19, 1994, with the birth of Addie Francys Williams. The slightly less than two years between the births of Cale and Addie was a period of major decline in Shirley's physical abilities. I was in a position to be involved with Cale as an infant to a degree not possible with Addie. Going to Pearsall when Cale or Kristi was ill, or bringing Cale to Kerrville for a day or so of playtime provided ample opportunity for me to be present as he discovered the world. It also included the other aspects of caring for a baby: changing diapers, feeding, bathing, and rocking. By the time of Addie's arrival, care for Shirley took up much of my energy and time. Shirley's one good kidney was failing, and the excess waste in her blood created weakness. Simply getting out of bed was a chore for Shirley.

Two months before Addie's birth, Shirley began hemodialysis. It cleaned her blood, but the process was not kind. We adjusted to the three trips per week to San Antonio. However, the three and one-half hour treatments took their toll. Shirley's blood pressure jumped from high to low. She had a seizure and numerous trips to emergency rooms. For many kidney failure patients, hemodialysis is a God send. It was not so for Shirley. Dr. Hura arranged for Shirley to be placed on a kidney transplant list. The pager provided to us by the transplant hospital gave us the good news on April 20, 1995. A match was on its way. A toddler had drowned in a swimming pool. An unspeakable tragedy for a family in Florida was a blessing for Shirley and me. Shirley received the small, healthy kidney the day after the pager message. Shirley was in the hospital for about two months due to complications with the surgery and the adjustments in antirejection medications. It took about six months for everything to stabilize and for the transplanted kidney to grow to match Shirley's body. She then felt better than she had in years. Clean blood did not bring back Shirley's youth, but she enjoyed Cale and Addie in ways not possible before the transplant.

***

In the fall of 1997 Annie fell while carrying her grill from the patio back to the garage. There were no broken bones, but she needed assistance. I drove Shirley to Hereford. The trip is a special memory as three-year-old Addie went with us. Kristi had brought her well-prepared daughter to Kerrville, and Addie had a complete set of play cooking utensils along with play dishes. Addie was on a mission to feed Maw-maw back to health. The imaginary food may not have done the trick, but Addie's delight in preparation and serving brought many smiles.

Addie and I left Hereford after a couple of days, while Shirley remained behind. We departed at 5am with Addie asleep in her car seat securely anchored in the middle of the rear seat. She did not arise until we came to San Angelo, where we ate breakfast. Sights and sounds as perceived by the inquisitive mind of a three-year-old made for a pleasurable road trip. When Addie spotted a park with swings and slide, we stopped. I believe there were four such parks. She found a quarter in the parking lot of the Dairy Queen where we had lunch. Addie took a short nap in the early afternoon. When we arrived in Pearsall, Addie was tired but not fussy. It had been a great day.

Annie's second fall was much worse. She broke a hip when she missed a stool while attempting to sit at her breakfast bar. Shirley was with her and called an ambulance to transport Annie to Lubbock for surgery. From the hospital, Annie was moved to Highland Medical Center for rehabilitation. The trauma was too great. Annie died on June 18, 1998. The last of Shirley's and my parents was gone.

***

Shirley stayed active until the early part of the twenty-first century. In the year 2000 we flew to Chicago to watch Jennifer Hubbard play in the Women US Open Golf Tournament. Jennifer was the daughter of Doug and Jackie. The Hubbards were friends from our years in San Antonio. Shirley was able to follow Jennifer on the course with the aid of an electric scooter. While in the Chicago area, Shirley relived the good times by visiting with Sally Steinkamp.

In the summer of 2002, Shirley was the host of a Dimmitt High School Reunion for all classes from the nineteen fifties. The Gunter Hotel in San Antonio was Shirley's selection for the location. Bonnie operated a catering business, and helped Shirley. It was a busy time. I created a website and handled all of the mailings. Shirley worked hard with planning the details. It would have been a herculean task even if Shirley had been in excellent health. The reunion went well, and Shirley was very pleased. I think her greatest pleasure was showing off Cale and Addie to her classmates. Our grandchildren handed out door prizes at the closing dinner of the reunion.

In early 2003 after eight years, Shirley's body finally rejected the transplanted kidney. Times were tough. She went through the very painful surgery of the installation of a subclavian port and began hemodialysis again. Shirley's reaction to hemodialysis was even worse than eight years earlier. Our only option was peritoneal dialysis. Shirley had to have a soft catheter placed in her abdomen. The catheter was used to fill her abdomen with a cleansing liquid. Waste products then passed from her blood through the abdominal lining. The filling and draining process was done at home. Shirley and I took training classes to learn the skills. We first used the manual process which required exchange of the dialysis fluids four times a day. The drain and refill process took forty-five minutes. One was done right before bedtime and another first thing in the morning. The two other exchanges during the day were separated by three hours. Shirley's lack of strength necessitated my doing the process. It became much easier after getting an automated cycler. It performed three to five exchanges during the night while Shirley slept. Peritoneal dialysis worked better for Shirley than hemodialysis. But that is like saying the filling of a tooth is less painful than a root canal. The daily grind was physically and emotionally exhausting. I remember a couple of poignant moments. One evening near bedtime

I was in my recliner reading the newspaper, and Shirley in her rocker when she sadly said, "Robert, it is getting so tiresome not being able to do anything."

Trying to be upbeat, I jokingly quipped, "What would you like to do? Go climb Mt. Everest."

"All I want is to stand and walk by myself to the bedroom."

My broken heart ached for how a cruel disease had crushed the will of a once long-suffering spirit. I did not let her see me cry, but the tears flowed when I was alone. A few weeks later in somewhat the same setting, Shirley said, "If I were not such a coward, I would give up and let it end."

A three-digit number on a thermometer is never good, but it is particularly bad for a person with a peritoneal catheter. I helped Shirley into our Yukon XL. We had given up our sedan because it had become very difficult for me to get Shirley in and out of such a low-to-ground vehicle. We rushed to the transplant hospital in San Antonio. There we received the sad but anticipated diagnosis. Shirley had a major infection, and peritoneal dialysis was no longer possible. Shirley was given only two options: a subclavian port for hemodialysis or hospice. She said no to the port which was not exactly saying yes to hospice. But the outcome was the same.

"Shirley, are you sure about hospice?"

"I think so. Besides, what's the difference?"

I had no adequate response. There were no words to counter the harsh reality of Shirley's rhetorical question.

"I will do what you wish, but please remember that we have been through difficult times before."

I called Kristi. She was there in less than an hour. Kristi counseled with her mother in a serious but subdued manner. Shirley didn't have a desire to die. However, she had experienced life down the hemodialysis path, and it had been horrid. This time there would not be a transplant off ramp, just an agonizing longer journey leading to the same end as the pain-free hospice route.

Shirley's decision contained a trace of doubt, a touch of rationale, and a ton of courage.

***

I was in the process of getting us ready for sleep in the early evening before Shirley's death. She wanted Vaseline on her lips to keep them moist during the night.

"I can't find any Vaseline. Will Chap Stick be ok?"

"Yes."

"I will get you some Vaseline tomorrow."

This statement by me resulted in Shirley's question which began this book.

Our house in Kerrville in 1991 (Shirley and me to right)

Shirley, Kristi, Addie, Annie, Cale (Four Generations)

Addie, Cale, Shirley, me

Part Two
Growing Up

Chapter 17

Heritage

Haskell, Texas

June 26, 1900

Mr. R. F. Keen

My dear Bob

We arived here Saturday eve. They all seemed to be glad to see us and of course we was glad to see them. Andrew Buford was here when we got here. Andrew, Hulda, Alf & I went to singing Sunday eve we enjoyed ourselves very well but I am afraid I'm not going to like the people's ways out here much although they are awful friendly but they are to wild the boys ride wild horses on Sunday and of course we are not used to that but we will have to try to make the best of it we can.

I guess we will put up our tent tomorrow Papa went after it yesterday Papa had his freight sent to Stamford that is the nearest R.R. station is about 14 miles from Haskell. This is a nice looking country but it is awful dry now.

Well I will try to ans. your last letter I rec'd in limestone of course I can live in the house with your Sisters and think I will enjoy it so much. I know we can get along alright I always did get along with every one I have lived with and I know we can get along alright so don't be uneasy about any thing like that Now Bob don't think I will want be "boss" at all for I never have been and I would not know what to do if I had to be. Well Bob you will have to excuss me this time I'm so bothered I can't think of much to write. Now please write soon and long to your loving sweetheart

Mary E. Draper

Spur, Tex. 7/26/1910

Dear Mary,

While we rest after dinner, I'll write you a few lines.

We have just had dinner. Had chicken too. Turned our chicks out with the others soon as we got here. They think they're at home. Have eat only 2 of them.

We are well & doing fine. Harvey & I are helping the others build first & they will help us. We all live together in the crib. They had the crib up when we got here. We are getting pretty well started on the big house. Making 4 room house. 2 rooms 14x14 and 20ft L for dinning room & kitchen. dinning room 12x14 kitchen 8x14. Hip roof all around. Have started a well. Haven't got much done on it. We have water from the little well done in the creek. Water is right good except it's warm. Haven't had rain enough to do much *good here yet. There is still stock water in the creek. We went to the plum orchard over on Cottonwood creek Sun. Got pail of plums. Paul & Hulda went after plums yesterday. Got nice lot of them. We eat dinner at Hulda's Sat. as we came. Harvey & I haven't bo't our lumber yet. It will cost about 130 or 140 dols each for our houses. Mr. D's cost about $200. Well Mary, we are so busy I can't write much. Did you get my card? Write to me every day or two. Haven't heard from home since I left. You know I soon get anxious to hear. How is Jack & the girls? Well I must go to work. I'm expecting a letter from you.*

As ever yours

Bob

These two letters were written by my maternal grandparents. I have attempted to type them exactly as written. The first was from my grandmother and sent to my grandfather before their marriage. The second was a letter my grandfather, Robert Fulton Keene, sent after their marriage. The spelling of the last name was changed sometime between 1910 and 1932. My grandmother wrote her letter just after her family's move from Limestone County, Texas to the community of Foster in Haskell County. The address section on the 114-year-old envelope with a two cent stamp in the upper right corner has three short lines. The first is *Mr R. F. Keen,* the second read *Burney,* and below the town is *Miss.* In the lower left corner my grandmother had written *Choctaw Co.* All was written using a graphite-lead pencil.

Mary Draper's family lived in Choctaw County, Mississippi prior to moving to Texas. She and my grandfather knew each other from childhood, and the relationship became romantic during a trip Mary made to Mississippi to visit family. Her letter is one of their courtship correspondences. Robert (Bob) and Mary wed on September 4, 1901, in Texas, but after marriage, they lived in Mississippi in the same house with Bob's sisters. The young couple moved to Texas sometime after August 16, 1904, the birthdate of my mother, Sallie Blanche Keene. The timing of my grandfather's letter was when the Caprock-South Plains area of Texas was changing from ranching to farming. Both sets of my grandparents were in the farming vanguard.

Eight months before Bob wrote the above letter to Mary, another young man arrived in the area of Spur, Texas. In October of 1909 William Fike (Jack) Godfrey from Paducah camped on the Spade draw. Jack at age twenty-three had come early for the big event scheduled for November 1, 1909.

> *E. P. Swenson and his associates purchased the Spur Ranch in 1907 and began subdividing the land for sale to settlers. Charles Adam Jones, then manager of the Spur interest, played the leading role in persuading Daniel Willard, head of the Burlington Railroad, to route a proposed railway line northwest from Stamford through the future site of Spur. On November 1, 1909, the first train of the Stamford and Northwestern passed through the new depot at Spur as the town was opened. Over 600 lots had been sold.*[4]

Jack purchased one of the 600 lots.

"A bunch of us were camped on the

---

[4] http://www.tshaonline.org/handbook/online/articles/hjs24

*Spade draw, 1/2 mile south of town,"
Godfrey recalls. "One night there was a
big rain and we were flooded out. Water
of half knee deep in our tents. We
dressed hastily, rolled up our pants,
and walked into town."*

*The Mahons, who had come here from
back east to put in a hotel, had a small
temporary building located somewhere
near the railroad. Jack moved in with
them and slept and ate there for a
while.*

*On the day of the opening, the sale of
lots were brisk, and averaged a lot a
minute.*

*"I bought the lot where Bell's Cafe is
now located, and put up a frame, 25x60
ft. building there." Godrey states.*

*The building was divided into three
partitions, one for a barber shop rented
to a Mr. Tidwell; one to a real estate
office; and the other for an insurance
office and sleeping quarters.*

*On the same day, Godfrey sold the
building to Charles Hamilton of Austin,
Texas, clearing a profit of $2,800.[5]*

Jack, an older brother of my paternal
grandmother, Anna Godfrey Baldwin, became a
prominent citizen of Spur. Thus, I had ancestors from
both sides of my family living near each other in 1910:
one a risk-taking merchant and the other a

[5]http://www.rootsweb.ancestry.com/~txdicken/spur
/g/godfrey_wf_kate.html

sodbuster/farmer. Each needed the other for the row-crop economy of West Texas to take hold and survive. Of course, all were dependent on rain.

When my grandfather and the other men finished building the houses and got wells dug, it was time for the families to move from Haskell County to Dickens County a distance of about seventy miles. The caravan consisted of two covered wagons, a buggy, and some horse-back riders who drove the milk cows. The trip took about a week.[6] My mother was almost six years old. Except for one year back in Mississippi, Mother spent the next fifteen years in Dickens County, the last seven in the community of Espuela. Espuela was about ten miles north of Spur. I will let Mother tell you about one of her happy memories of life in Dickens County.

The events that happened during that year were not that unusual for a family living on a cotton farm. One special thing was the Draper Family Reunion on July 4th. We went to the Spur Ranch for an all-day picnic. It was a nice place to have a celebration. The buildings were down in a canyon near a stream of running water, so there were lots of large shade trees. We had home-made ice cream and lots of other good things to eat. There was a windmill in the canyon that was twice as high as regular ones so that it could get the benefit of the wind above the cliff of the canyon. Of course, this became a challenge for several of us to see who could climb to the top. One special remembrance of that day was that we had some group pictures made by a big

_____

[6] *Wherever He Leads* by Blanche Keene Baldwin, page 12

*barn. A few years ago this same barn
was moved to Lubbock and is one of the
buildings in the Ranching Heritage
Center of the Texas Tech University
Museum. Each time I have visited the
Museum, I am reminded of the
wonderful celebrations we had in by-
gone times.[7]*

In 1925 the family moved a little farther west.
Again I will step aside and let Mother tell you about the
relocation.

*As the years passed living at Espuela,
our family's financial obligations had
advanced sufficiently enough that Papa
thought the time was right to invest in
some land for a home. So the urge to
move on West seemed to be in order. At
that time, Papa went out to the wide
open spaces west of Lubbock to the
new town of Levelland, in Hockley
County. That part of the country was
just settling up since some of the ranch
country was being divided and sold for
farming purposes. The preparations for
making a move to another location were
carried out throughout the entire
year....Through the summer we carried
on with regular routine things, then
when the crops were laid by, Papa
made preparations to go to Levelland.
After equipping three covered wagons
with the supplies necessary for a
camping-out trip, Papa, Draper, Myrna,
and Viola began the journey to the
West....They were on the road for a*

---

[7] *Wherever He Leads* by Blanche Keene Baldwin, pages 26 & 27

week....Draper, Myrna, and Viola helped Papa build a three-room house on the new place which was about eight miles south of Levelland in the Clauene Community. They had a well drilled and put up a windmill and made some other improvements. Meanwhile Mama, Doss, and I were left at home to keep things under control and do the farm work.

...When moving day came and the time for loading the two wagons with all of the household things and other belongings for moving, there were several thoughtful friends and neighbors who came to help with the work....In January of 1925, Papa and Draper left with the wagons. They made the trip in five days without any trouble. The rest of us went in the car with George as the driver. He was just thirteen years of age, but that was before driver's licenses were required. It was a day's trip for us....We passed through Lubbock, which did not appear to cover a very large area at that time. We then drove by the few buildings of the new college of Texas Tech that was just being built. The college location seemed to be a long way west of the town.[8]

A note of clarification: Mother's brother George was also called Doss.

There is only one generation between me and my ancestors who ploughed up small lots of ranch grassland for farming. First it was Dickens County and

---

[8] *Wherever He Leads* by Blanche Keene Baldwin, pages 45-47

later Hockley County.

***

In the early spring of 2012, I stopped in front of a house at 1105 Southeast Fourth Avenue in Mineral Wells, Texas. The white clapboard house needed painting and some repairs but was not dilapidated. There was a small satellite television dish in the front-right yard nearer to the street than to the house. My objective was to see if the house still existed. Since its condition was not so bad, I had a desire to go inside and walk the floors once trod by my ancestors. A barking dog stood near the left corner of the structure. No other signs of occupancy were apparent. A woman and a teenaged boy were in the yard of the house next door to the north.

"Excuse me, do you know if anybody lives here," I asked while gesturing toward the house.

The woman replied, "I'm not sure. It was vacant, but I think some squatters are there now. I'm pretty sure they have no water or power."

"Do you know who owns it?"

"No, my son and I have been here less than a year."

"It was my great grandfather's home many years ago. Do you think it would be ok for me to knock on the door and see if anyone answers? I would like to see the inside."

"It should be ok. I will go with you, if you want."

"No, you and your son stand by to call 911 if someone comes out with a shotgun," I replied with a grin.

No one responded to my knocking. I thanked the woman, snapped a couple of pictures, and departed.

My great grandfather, John Milton Baldwin, died in that house at six o'clock Wednesday evening Friday July 7, 1927. John Milton was born in Hawkins County, Tennessee in 1855 and came to Texas at the age of twenty-nine. He must have been a successful farmer since he was able to retire at age fifty-eight. His retirement could also have been precipitated by the loss of his right leg just above the knee. Therefore, he did not drive, nor did my great grandmother, Minerva. They had a black, chauffeur-driven Studebaker to ferry them around. One of John Milton's three sons followed his lead and became a farmer. Byron King Baldwin, my grandfather, was the farming son. I do not know how my Baldwin grandparents met. It could have been when they were young as both the Baldwin and Godfrey families lived in Cottle County near Paducah.

Family legend relates that the Godfreys felt Anna had better choices than Byron King Baldwin. Anna and her siblings were educated. Thressia, Anna's sister, received a Bachelor of Arts Degree from Hardin-Simmons on June 3, 1914. Of the thirty-nine graduates, twenty-one were females. My grandmother Baldwin also attended Hardin-Simmons but did not complete her degree requirements.

The Granddaddy Baldwin I knew had a kind, gentle nature. He was a hard working dry-land cotton farmer. My grandmother must have seen some of the same fine characteristics when he was young that I observed in his later years. My father, Byron Howard Baldwin, was the first-born of the union between Byron King and Anna. Daddy had eight siblings who lived to adulthood. I do not know the exact movements of my Baldwin grandparents when my father was a child. But when he was a young man attending Wayland College in Plainview, his family was farming near the new community of Sundown. The Baldwins began attending the Fellowship Baptist Church just north of Clauene where the Keenes (including my mother) were members.

It was there my parents first met and later married on July 21, 1929.

Both of my grandmothers were strong, independent women but with different personalities. Grandmother Baldwin was very outgoing and direct. If the world was a stage, then my paternal grandmother's stage was larger and more diverse than my grandmother Keene's. But each played the lead in their separate productions.

My memories of Granddaddy Keene are limited. He was bedridden at the time of my first recollection. I have been told he was soft-spoken with a keen but gentle sense of humor. I enjoyed my Granddaddy Baldwin. He died in our house at the age of sixty-four. It is my first memory of being present at a death. I inherited a tremor from him. Hopefully, I also have his kindness gene. Daddy was more like his mother, and Mother more akin to her father. I have always been told I veer slightly towards my Keene heritage, especially in physical appearance.

My Keene grandparents (Robert Fulton & Mary Eualine Draper) on their wedding day September 4, 1901

House of my great-grandfather John Milton Baldwin

Mother and Daddy (1953)

Chapter 18

Childhood

I am a product of the area around Lubbock, Texas, USA—every bit as much as a bale of cotton, a combine-hopper of maize, or a spectacular sunset. Neither my childhood environment nor I was one-dimensional. The South Plains was also home of dust storms, goat-head stickers, and crop-destroying hail.

While employed by the Bell System, I was sent to Ames, Iowa for a winter term at Iowa State in the nineteen seventies. My classmates were all from Bell System entities. One was a young man from Long Island, New York. He approached me and said, "Robert, I see from the class roster that you graduated from Texas Tech."

"Yes, I did."

"I always wanted to meet someone from Lubbock, Texas."

"Why?"

"When I was about ten years old, my father thought it a good idea to drive our family from Long Island to California. I vividly remember the drive across Texas, and I have a question for you."

"Ok." I said wondering.

"First there is nothing, and then there is Lubbock. After Lubbock, there is nothing again. How did Lubbock get there?"

I was embarrassed by my lack of knowledge of Lubbock's history. I was able to respond, "I am not sure, but I suspect Tech being there helped."

I still do not have a complete answer. My answer back then had merit. But if asked the question now, I would speak of my grandparents and other dry-land cotton farmers like them who built their houses by hand, broke the sod, planted the seed, and prayed for rain. Their combined meager successes and the resulting support of small businesses, paved the way for Lubbock to survive and later thrive with the advent of deep-well irrigation. Today one big question is, "If the water plays out, what will happen to Lubbock and the agribusinesses associated with King Cotton?"

***

I have no direct memory of living in New Mexico, the state of my birth. In fact there is little during the first year or so in Texas that I am sure is my first-hand memory versus being told after the fact. But there is an item for which I am positive the real incidents are imprinted on my brain. It concerns my mother and my name. Mother had a non-confrontational, soft-spoken personality, but if she heard someone address me as *Bob,* she would say in a polite, firm tone, "His name is *Robert.* If I had wanted him to be called *Bob,* I would have named him *Bob.*"

***

The locations of my childhood were: Lorenzo, Robertson, Idalou, and Woodrow. Each was different but with certain similarities. There were no traffic signals unless a main highway went through; each had a school, a small store, a cotton gin, two or three churches (Baptist, Methodist, and sometimes a Church of Christ), and houses for the teachers, ministers, and other residents. If anyone said he was going to town, everyone knew he was headed to Lubbock, the Hub of the South Plains. The social and economic structure was similar in all four towns. As a child it seemed as if gaps between each level were huge. But in reality except for the lowest couple of strata there were slight differences in a basic sameness. The hierarchy was topped by families who owned and farmed debt-free land. But there were few of these since most land owners had a note with a bank in Lubbock. These with notes on their land formed the third level just below the gin and mercantile store owners. The fourth group was where my family fit: school administrators, ministers, and a few professionals who commuted to Lubbock. Below us were farmers who leased their land and the classroom teachers. Next were the families who worked for the land-owning farmers, some blue-collar workers, and school maintenance and clerical staff. There were a few who scratched out a living doing odd jobs, and the last were the migrant farm workers.

Daddy seldom did school and church work in the same community. In the four towns listed, he was employed by the school district—mostly as the high school principal. Only in Robertson was he also the pastor of the Baptist church. He pastored in even smaller communities of Becton and Estacado where the Baptists had the only church. Community activities revolved around the church. Only as an adult did I fully comprehend the influence of my father. He had the undivided attention of most all residents three times per week—on Wednesday nights and twice on Sundays.

***

I was a few days past my sixth birthday in late August 1944 when I enrolled in the first grade in Lorenzo Elementary School. My family no longer lived in

Lorenzo. Daddy was still employed by the Lorenzo school district, but he was also pastor of the Baptist church in Robertson. The church in Robertson owned a house in which we lived rent free. My three older sisters and older brother began the school year in Robertson. I rode with Daddy to Lorenzo each school day. The arrangement lasted only a couple of months until Daddy was made principal and coach for Robertson High School. So I changed schools during first grade. My first day in the classroom at Robertson is well remembered. I didn't know where the restroom was and was too intimidated to ask. You guessed it. I peed in my pants. The floor was not level, so it ran toward the front of the room.

Idalou was my school for grade two. Daddy was Idalou's high school principal. I don't recall much of that year. We lived in a school-district owned house adjacent to the school buildings. I had the mumps or measles and when feeling better, I hollered out the window to my friends on the playgrounds. I went to Idalou about five years ago, and the house was still there.

Third grade began with another change of schools. Cooper Elementary School located in the community of Woodrow about ten miles south of Lubbock was my school for the next four years. I enjoyed the time in Woodrow very much. This is not to imply that living in Lorenzo, Robertson, and Idalou was unpleasant. Quite the contrary, all my growing up years were more pleasurable than not. In Woodrow we lived in one of the half-dozen or so teachers' housing. Those houses were referred to as *Rat Row*. Originally it may have been a pejorative term, but we used it with pride. Mr. Johns, the school maintenance man, had children near our ages. I was the fifth of seven children, so I always had playmates. My three brothers and my youngest sister, Olagene (Ola), were still in elementary school. My two older sisters, Mary and Wynelle, were in high school. Therefore, they ran in different circles in our small Woodrow universe. Ola went into high school our second year in the Cooper schools—one less playmate. But there were always enough for a good game of tag, ante-over, or kick-the-can. Godfrey was able to entertain himself. Eugene seldom felt too young to play with us. He was tough, but being the youngest; at times he would end up crying. Mother would simply advise him not to play with the older children.

Almost everyone in the town of Woodrow and the rural area around soon knew Daddy, Mary, and Wynelle. At functions involving a large number of people, I would often have the following type of conversation:

"Are you one of the Baldwin boys?" a stranger would ask.

"Yes."

"I know Darold is the oldest son and Eugene the youngest. Are you the second or third?" was apt to be the next question. It was seldom, "Are you Robert or Godfrey?"

To secure my top spot in the middle, my usual response was, "I am Robert, the next-to-oldest son."

***

Daddy was half-time pastor for both Becton and Estacada churches. He preached at one on the first and third Sundays and the other on the second and fourth Sundays. On fifth Sundays the family would worship at the Woodrow Baptist Church. Mary and Wynelle attended at Woodrow every Sunday so as to be with friends. Ola followed suit when she entered high school. Darold and I also did the same after a couple of years. I was baptized in the Woodrow church.

Growing Up
***

In the fall when the cotton was ready for harvest, it took all available hands to do the job. School would dismiss at noon to allow students to work in the cotton patches. For cotton boll-pulling, young age was not a disqualification. The farmers paid by weight, $1.75 per 100 pounds. Therefore, since age 8 I could drag the small cotton sack which was sewed by Mother, get it to the spring-scales for weighing, crawl up into the trailer with the full sack, and empty it, I picked cotton. I had my first paying job in the fall of my third year of school. I do not remember my output capabilities at age eight, but by twelve or thirteen I could do 300 pounds in a school-day afternoon and 500 to 600 pounds on a Saturday.

After a quick lunch we kids in *Rat Row* would meet beside the dirt road in front of our houses with our sacks, straw hats, gloves, and burlap-wrapped canning jars filled with water, and wait for a farmer to pick us up. We would all climb into the bed of the pickup and head to the cotton fields for an afternoon of boll-pulling. I liked being paid based on output not time spent, since I was a pretty good boll-puller. At the end of the first cotton harvest I took my earnings, and with Daddy's help opened my first bank account. From it, I purchased my school clothes and had spending money. I had a better deal than Mary and Wynelle as their first earnings went into the family budget. They worked at Mark Halsey Drug Store Number One. At noon on Saturdays, there was live music by Hop Halsey, grandson of Mark Halsey the owner, and The Drug Store Cowboys. The music was broadcast on KFYO radio station and Mark's son was the master of ceremony of a contest called *Scavenger's Ante*. He would give a silver dollar to the first person who brought him the item he requested (i.e. a shoe lace or a 1940 nickel.) The drug store had a railed balcony area where the band played, and it was from there we younger children witnessed the fun below. I loved it—especially hearing my sisters call out the slang names for the soda fountain drink orders, such as *Draw One* for coffee or *A Squeeze* for orange juice. It made me feel as if I were part of some secret order.

In addition to being an educator and a minister, Daddy also obtained an electrician's license. When not going to Texas Tech during the summer, he did electrical work for the farmers and other people in town. Darold helped him, and if a job was big enough, I was the *gofer*. Part of my job was to pull wires in tight spots. I got stuck a couple of times. Once, under a pier-and-beam house which panicked me, Daddy calmed me by talking through the floor while Darold got near enough to move enough dirt to free me. Pay for electrical work was also better than boll-pulling.

***

Lubbock had a semipro baseball team called the Hubbers. Daddy would take his sons and our friends to the games. The ball park had chicken-wire to protect the stands behind home plate. Cables holding the wire sloped from the ground to a height of about thirty feet in front of the bleachers, and then were level with the ground over the top of the people watching the action. During one game two popped-up balls went high and landed in the level area just above our heads. There they stayed. The Lubbock Hubbers were low budget, and leaving two good baseballs on the chicken-wire was not an option. A ticket-taker used a long cane pole without results. Daddy went to the young man and said something we boys did not hear. The two of them then went to the ticket booth and met with an older man.

Daddy came and told me to come with him. We went to the top row of the stands where the wire netting stopped. There Daddy said, "I told the man if they would give you a free ticket for another game, you would retrieve the balls."

"Ok, but how am I going to get them?"

Daddy then explained, "I will lift you up to where you can get on top of the wire covering. Once there you crawl on your stomach above one of the supporting cables out to the ball nearest us and then keep part of your weight on the cable while you stretch out and get that ball. After you get it, move all your weight back over the cable and pitch the ball to the sloped part of the chicken-wire. Then, crawl down to the other ball and do the same. When you're finished, crawl back here by following the cable, and I will help you down."

While I was moving toward the first ball, the umpire stopped play, and all eyes were on me. The crowd was quiet until the fingers of my stretched-out right hand grasped the first ball, and then all cheered. The cheers turned to boos when I pitched the ball so that it rolled down the sloping wire into the catcher's mitt. The fans were again silent as I made my way to the second ball. After I got the other ball, a man shouted, "Keep it kid. You earned it." No one booed when I tossed the ball toward home plate. There was a standing ovation as I crawled back, and Daddy helped me down.

***

I will close this chapter by trying to do the impossible—write an objective narrative about some of my inherited traits. They include attributes for which I am neither proud nor ashamed. In some incidents, they were assets and other times liabilities. All the traits were present at birth and are still part of who I am seventy-five years later. This chapter titled *Childhood* seems as good as any for their discussion.

One is curiosity. The other two each have an element of contradiction. I have the ability for a concentrated focus on a single thing, but I also can embrace diversity of thought. This is not to suggest I am good at multitasking. Quite the opposite, my brain can handle input only in sequence. One result is being absent-minded. The last trait concerns tidiness—this should not to be confused with cleanliness. If you could see the inside of my automobile and my office filing system, I doubt you would think the same person had responsibility for both. In the first there is chaos and organization in the other. The combination of these qualities has at times made it both frustrating and amusing to be around me. Sunday mornings as a child, I put all the above on display. Each of my older sisters had the responsibility of getting a younger brother ready for church. Wynelle was unlucky and had me. Getting me ready was not difficult. I don't want to brag, but I cleaned up nicely. I liked how I looked when Wynelle completed the finishing touch of combing my hair. The problem occurred when she began to get herself ready. My curiosity often led me outside where I would focus on some activity which destroyed all of Wynelle's fine efforts. But she found the solution. One Sunday morning after getting me ready Wynelle told me, "Young man, march yourself into the living room, set yourself down in a chair, and don't you dare get out of the chair until time to get into the car." That became the routine each Sunday until I was old enough to dress myself.

In my early years if a small item of Mother's was not in its proper place, she came first to me and asked, "Robert, do you have my thimble?"

"No ma'am."

"Check your pockets, please."

I was always surprised to find it there, but Mother never was.

Mary, Wynelle, Olagene, Eugene, me, Darold, Godfrey
(1944)

Darold, me, Eugene, Godfrey, Wynelle, Mary, Ola (2014)

Chapter 19

Adolescence

The nineteen fifties was a decade to remember: teenage years, the advent of television, rock 'n roll, auto tail fins, Mad Magazine, and development of good study habits.

In late August of 1950 I walked into the Wellman Elementary School building to enter the seventh grade. A new school and new friends were to be embraced, not dreaded. My casual attitude concerning report card grades was a distant memory. I had been allowed to pass from third to fourth grade at Cooper on the condition of my attending summer school at Dupre Elementary in Lubbock. That near failure transformed me into a dedicated student. At Wellman my marks were good.

Wellman, a small town of about 200 residents, was twelve miles southwest of Brownfield, the seat of Terry County. It was an hour's drive from Lubbock. It was during the five years at Wellman I changed from childhood to the cusp of young manhood. When we left Woodrow, there were three older siblings at home. The last year at Wellman I was the oldest child in the house. For the first time, I had a bed to myself—not just a bed but an entire room. I felt spoiled as Mother and Daddy bought me an electric blanket—the only one in the house. Mother would turn it on when she went to bed on cold nights when I played out-of-town football or basketball games. I can still feel the warm inviting comfort of crawling under that blanket after a long ride in a cold school bus.

***

There were two exciting periods for me during the 1950-1951 school year. One was football in the fall and the other, the Terry County Meet in the spring.

Wellman had its first-ever football team in the fall of 1950. The excitement this created cannot be over stated. For good or bad small towns and cities in Texas were—and still are—defined by their football teams. A side anecdote may help illustrate this point.

Tascosa High School in Amarillo had good football teams during each of the five years I taught there. Two years they advanced to the state semifinals in the largest school classification. Both of these years, Tascosa was eliminated by the state champion. The time period was the nineteen sixties at the height of a youth rebellion—mostly on university campuses but also in high schools. At Tascosa, such unrest was muted; it consisted mostly of an underground newsletter. I don't remember its title, and the students who published it were not known—at least by me. A new edition hit the hallways in a cloud of mystery about once a month. It was read by all to see who got lampooned. The writers were clever. Their favorite targets were school policies, administrators, teachers, popular students, and jocks—especially football players. My name was never mentioned. I'm not sure if that was a compliment or an insult. A section in each issue was a list of words and phrases with the publishers' definition. One read as follows: *A football pep rally is a religious service where those in attendance worship thirty gods, not just one.*

Wellman was ready for the sacred Friday night games by the time our family moved into a house on teachers' row. The temple...I mean stadium... had been constructed recently. It was modest. But recall there were less than a hundred students in high school. There were wooden bleachers on the west side of the field which would hold about two hundred fans. There was no seating on the east side. People would simply watch from their cars parked facing the playing field. The field was lighted but just barely sufficiently so. A new field house containing two dressing rooms with showers and separate restrooms for the spectators stood near the west corner of the south end zone. A concession stand and separate ticket booth were located near the entry gate. The home team's dressing room included the coach's office and a well-stocked equipment room. None of the pads had ever been used.

I was the only player on the elementary school team who was able to get all the gear on without help from Coach Walser. I had played football at Cooper. When we gathered in the south end zone for the initial team meeting, Coach Walser addressed his collection of excited but scared sixth, seventh, and eighth graders with these opening words, "Is there anyone who has played football before?" I was the only one who raised a hand. "You are my quarterback." This was the first step of my one claim-to-fame as a football player.

That first year of play, the high school team did not win a game. I don't recall how many games the elementary school team played. But we had lost them all until the last game, which was against Meadow. We ran a split-T formation with me under center, who was Bob Womack. I normally took the ball and moved a step or two to the right or left and handed the ball to either Burke Slaughter or Leon Abbott. My normal cadence count at the line-of-scrimmage was, "Down...Set...Hut one...Hut two...Hut three." Early during the game with Meadow, I called, "Thirty-five on one." Burke Slaughter broke free for a touchdown. We did not score the extra point, but no matter. We were ahead by six to zip. It was not a familiar situation for us. For the remainder of the game, Meadow kept us pinned with our backs near our own goal line. But we managed to keep Meadow from scoring a touchdown. Oh, by the way, they did tackle me twice for safeties. However, with less than three minutes to play we had the ball on our thirty-yard line and were ahead six to four. Daddy was officiating the game. It was not uncommon for an assistant high school coach of the home team to officiate an elementary game. I was so excited that I used poor play-clock management. At the end of a play, as I hurried back to the huddle, Daddy walked up close to me and said, "Slow down, Son." I took my time calling the play and told the guys to walk, not run, to the line-of-scrimmage. Bob giggled as I called the signals, Dooown...... Seeet...... Huut...... Onne...... Huut. We kept the ball until time expired. Thus, I was the quarterback of the first Wellman football team to win a game. In the year 2000 there was a celebration of Wellman's (now Wellman-Union) fifty years of football. Darold was one of the high school team members to attend. In a telephone conversation with Leon Abbott concerning the event, he reminded me, "Robert, you were the first quarterback from Wellman to win a game." That *honor* is forever.

Bob Womack and I worked the concession stands for the high school games. Coke provided a metal container twenty inches long, ten inches wide, and ten inches deep. It had a leather strap attached to each end that was placed around the neck and held the container at waist level. A slight curve in the container made it easy to carry. It held about a dozen glass bottles of soda-pop; Coke, RC, Nehi Orange, and 7 Up which were cooled with crushed ice. I believe the price was a nickel. Bob and I made the rounds of the cars surrounding the playing field. There was a bottle opener on the right end of the container. After the games, we picked up the refillable empties, and placed them in a wooden crate which had slots for twenty-four bottles.

***

The Terry County Meet of 1951 was a happy event for me. A county meet was a time where students in the seventh and eighth grades of elementary schools in a county had interschool scholastic and athletic competition. The meet was held at Brownfield High School in early May.

Mr. Walser came into our classroom and said, "We need someone for Junior Declamation at county meet. Who wants to try out?" No hands were lifted. "Oh, I forgot to mention that the student selected will be excused from English class between now and the meet in order to practice." I think every hand went up, including mine. The word *junior* in the title meant the contest was for seventh-grade students. All eighth-grade activities were referred to as *senior* events.

I was chosen as Wellman's entry. It was a big thing in our house. Mother sewed my first suit. It was navy blue. Daddy showed me how to knot my tie. Olagene gave me a double check as I left the house to catch the bus, and she said, "Come home with a blue ribbon."

There were about ten other nervous junior declaimers backstage as we drew numbers. I pulled the next to last position. The size of the auditorium and the stillness of the large crowd could not be avoided. I stood alone for a few seconds at the microphone located at front-center stage. But the words came, "*The Children's Hour* by Henry Wadsworth Longfellow." After a slight pause as instructed by Mr. Walser during our practice sessions, I began,

> *"Between the dark and the daylight,*
> *When the night is beginning to lower,*
> *Comes a pause in the day's occupations,*
> *That is known as the Children's Hour.*
> *I hear in the chamber above me*
> *The patter of little feet,*

The sound of a door that is opened,
And voices soft and sweet.
From my study I see in the lamplight,
Descending the broad hall stair,
Grave Alice, and laughing Allegra,
And Edith with golden hair.
A whisper, and then a silence:
Yet I know by their merry eyes
They are plotting and planning together
To take me by surprise.
A sudden rush from the stairway,
A sudden raid from the hall!
By three doors left unguarded
They enter my castle wall!
They climb up into my turret
O'er the arms and back of my chair;
If I try to escape, they surround me;
They seem to be everywhere.
They almost devour me with kisses,
Their arms about me entwine,
Till I think of the Bishop of Bingen
In his Mouse-Tower on the Rhine!
Do you think, O blue-eyed banditti
Because you have scaled the wall,
Such an old mustache as I am
Is not a match for you all!
I have you fast in my fortress,
And will not let you depart,
But put you down into the dungeon
In the round-tower of my heart.
And there will I keep you forever,
Yes, forever and a day,
Till the walls shall crumble to ruin,
And moulder in dust away!"

I exited the stage to a standing ovation and knew
it had gone well. I wrapped the cord of the blue ribbon
around a button of my white shirt for all to see and
went to the stadium to watch my friends doing track

and field. But mostly I wanted to make sure they saw my prize. Fame is fickle as the next year I came in second with only five contestants in Senior Declamation.

***

Oil and water do not mix. But if the oil was from a royalty-producing pump-jack and the water from a deep well with an eight-inch pipe stream which quenched rain-starved fields of cotton, their combination changed the social structure of a small community. Wellman had transformations in the first half of the 1950s so stark that even a sometimes clueless teenager like me took note. Terry County was in the oil-rich north Permian Basin, and oil was discovered in the 1940s. In 1950 over 780,000 barrels of petroleum were pumped out of Terry County lands. By 1956 oil production had jumped tenfold, reaching 7,463,320 barrels. During the same timeframe many farms changed from dry-land to irrigation. There was a hit or miss randomness concerning oil. The good fortune of having abundant water deep below the sandy-loam soil was more universal. The key word is *more* not *total*, as not all had water wells sufficient for crops. It was not uncommon to find families from contiguous farms where one had producing oil wells and the other nothing but dry holes. When this happened, the dynamics were altered quickly and permanently. Before oil both were dirt-poor, dry-land cotton farmers, and in the blink-of-an-eye one had relocated to a new ranch-style home in Lubbock while the other was still striving to fit the cost of a very used pickup into his budget.

The advent of oil and deep-well irrigation impacted not just the individuals directly involved but also the whole community. Wellman constructed a new high school building, and the school provided all students with supplies and athletic gear. I was shocked when at Hereford the players had to provide their own Converse All Stars, socks, gym shorts with tops, and jock straps. At Wellman there were two special perks for juniors who made the varsity basketball team. At the end of the season we were given one of the used game balls. I still have mine, and it holds air. But best of all the school paid all expenses for us to go to the boy's state basketball tournament played in Gregory Gymnasium on the campus of the University of Texas in Austin. There were three of us in 1955—Claude Chambers, Leon Abbott, and me. Coaches Sewell and Conwoop were our escorts. The five of us went in a driver-education automobile provided to the school by one of the dealerships in Brownfield. My enjoyment of that trip was almost beyond words. It instilled a desire to attend future tournaments. By age seventy-five, I had been to more than thirty-five. Cale started going with me when he was about ten years of age, but the venue was no longer in Gregory. During one of the early trips with Cale, we went to the still-standing old gym. There we stood at center court of the floor where years before his grandmother had played for two championship teams. I remember the results of the 1955 tournament better than the most recent one played in March 2014.

***

Daddy was ready, or at least he thought he was. The Zenith television set with a seventeen-inch screen had been purchased. A two-bay conical reception antenna was atop a thirty-foot, two-inch windmill pipe firmly attached to a threaded base pipe secured in concrete. There were three guy wires to keep it upright during sand storms. Daddy adjusted the facing direction by using a large pipe-wrench. It was pointed in the

194

direction of Lubbock. The final setting was determined by group consensus of the other men in town. It was Daddy's brain child but a whole town's project. Our television set was the first and only one in Wellman scheduled to be ready by 8pm Thursday November 13, 1952—the time and date of the beginning of television broadcasting in the South Plains. Lubbock Avalanche-Journal writer Kenneth May reported that first broadcast as a breaking news event:

> "Lubbock's first television station, KDUB-TV began broadcasting at exactly 8 p.m. Thursday as scores of area residents tripped the master switch which sent the opening ceremonies direct from Main and Texas Avenue into the living rooms of many South Plains homes." May added, "The station carried a 'live' broadcast from the outdoor stage until 9 p.m., and continued with films until 11:30 p.m. It will return to the video waves for several hours each day on an interim operation setup until its permanent home, now under construction, is completed in Southwest Lubbock."

Our living room was filled to overflowing with some on the outside who watched the small, snowy screen through the windows. The sound was not so bad, but the picture was mainly static. The Tech band played early in the live portion of the broadcast. While the music was playing, talk from our front-room audience consisted of statements like: "I think I see a drum." or "Isn't that a person's head?" There was a slight problem in Daddy's plan. The fault resulted from good intentions. He knew other teachers would soon want television. So he placed the antenna at a central location for all teacherages. This resulted in the lead wires being too long. This was soon corrected by placing the antenna pole adjacent to our house. Daddy also added another bay to the antenna and used larger gauge transmission wires. The Zenith proved to be important during my last year in Wellman. On Saturday nights we guys would cut our trips to Brownfield short in order to return to my house to watch TV. One of those nights Godfrey and Eugene placed a cat in Bob's car while he, Burke, and I were engrossed in a horror movie. Bob left just after midnight and had driven a short distance when the cat jumped upon the back of the car seat. Bob bailed out of the moving auto. Good thing the car was a stick shift as it quickly stopped.

***

Wellman in the nineteen fifties was a good time and place for the *coming-of-age* of a young boy. The values and work ethics were a solid base for a rewarding, stable adult life.

Me (age 17)

Part Three
Post 2004

Chapter 20

Empty House

"...The complete blood counts are normal. The white blood counts are normal in number and the cell types are of a...," Dr. Miller was giving me the report of my annual physical. The date was September 2, 2004, less than two months after Shirley's death.

I always had a comprehensive checkup near my birthday.

"...is normal with no signs of abnormal acidification of your...," the doctor continued. I had become accustomed to a good report.

"....I will skip the PSA number for now and discuss it with you at the end. Your total cholesterol is 131...." His voice faded from my awareness. The words and volume continued, but they were mere background noise as my mind was focused on the echo of, "...skip the PSA...and discuss it...at the end." *What did that mean?*

***

For the past few weeks, life had been a psychological bungee jump into a dark mental canyon— free fall toward fear of the unknown then suddenly yanked back to a feeling of "all will be fine." It was a repetitious cycle with my emotional elasticity placed under less stress with each progression. But, w*hen-oh-when will there be a new stability?* Intellectually I knew Shirley would die before me, but I was not ready emotionally for the reality. The house felt big and empty. I stayed busy—partly with the necessity of doing death-related paper work. Family and friends provided a good support base. But I felt a need for more. Local community grief groups were not a fit for me. Lengthy telephone conversations with friends whose spouses had recently died gave me the most comfort. Lewis Cobb and Mary Alice Moore Drake both helped during some of my lowest points.

***

"Robert, while your PSA is not outrageously high, it has been stable for so long that this increase indicates a need for you see a urologist."

"Whom would you recommend?" I inquired.

"Dr. Gene Smith—he is in this tower. I will have Delia make an appointment."

"Should I be concerned?"

"The probability is low for anything serious, but let's wait and see what Dr. Smith thinks."

***

What is normal in the abnormal? Shirley had been the center of my life for nearly half a century. What are appropriate feelings and actions? These were the thoughts which occupied my mind as I tried to gain my footing for life after Shirley. I don't remember ever considering the idea that my life was finished when Shirley died. I recollect well the feeling of loneliness and desire for companionship. I hated eating alone, enough so that if I saw a woman of my generation sitting alone, I would ask if I might join her. Only one said no, and she indicated a lack of time. I had many delightful conversations with interesting females and crossed paths with only one later. I asked a surprised Lois Ellis to eat with me while we stood in line at CiCi's Pizza one Friday night. The next time we saw each other was an unexpected encounter at Alto Frio Baptist Encampment.

My emotional well-being started to level out that fall. I took training as a hospice volunteer, and it was rewarding. If asked, I indicated no desire to remarry. I did not knowingly lie, but it was not the complete truth. At that time I was not sure what I wanted. However, I knew for sure that growing old alone was not my desire.

***

Dr. Smith did a biopsy of my prostate gland and gave me reassurance that the percentages were favorable and the results would be negative. Kristi accompanied me in early September to hear the results. *Prostate adenocarcinoma* were not the words we wanted nor expected to hear. The doctor's recommendation was radioactive seeds therapy. I agreed, and we scheduled a date for the implantation.

I telephoned Godfrey. He had been diagnosed with prostate cancer five years earlier, and he agreed to help me find the most current information. Godfrey said, "Robert, I know you, and in the end, there will not be adequate data for your comfort. I will help with the research but will not give advice." I understood. Godfrey was correct. For my age and Gleason Score, there was not a consensus as to the best therapy. I cancelled the procedure with Dr. Smith and made arrangements for a second opinion at MD Anderson Cancer Center in Houston.

***

There was not a clear image in my mind concerning relationships with the opposite sex. Reverting to a teenage mentality, dating was a place to start. Even though I was no longer a believer, I had retained the values of my youth. The greatest chance for compatibility would be a church-going woman. My friends, the McClintocks, were members of Trinity Baptist. I sought Carol's help. She gave me a couple of names with telephone numbers and indicated she had checked and a call from me would be welcome. Peggy Morrow was one of the names. "Robert, you may have seen Peggy's name and picture on for-sale signs in Kerrville since she is a successful real estate agent." I did not remember ever seeing one of Peggy's for-sale signs, but I checked her broker's web site. I left a voice mail on Peggy's telephone in early November.

***

My second-opinion appointment at MD Anderson was also in early November. I was scheduled for a battery of tests and then discussions with two doctors— one in surgical therapy and the other in radiation treatments. Both gave similar readouts. There was good news. The word *cure* was not used, but all possible options (except *wait and see*) provided a nearly certain guarantee that something other than prostate cancer would lead to my final demise. After a week of self-debate, I chose to have my gland surgically removed. The possibility of unpleasant side effects was offset by the high probability of removal of all the cancerous tissues. The scheduled date was December tenth, and the location was MD Anderson.

***

I was baking two pecan pies on a Saturday in late November when my telephone rang. The pies were for a dessert bake sale to support the youth programs of Cale and Addie's church. There was no name on the caller ID display. I answered the call with a simple, "Hello."

"Hello, this is Peggy Morrow, and I am returning your call." The name did not register with me immediately as my message had been left more than a week before. Peggy continued, "I am having an open house in your neighborhood, and no one is here at the moment." An introductory conversation between single males and females is different when the persons are older. The effort to make a good first impression is independent of age. But with age, an edge of polite directness creeps in. Within the first few minutes of our conversation, I asked, "Are you widowed or divorced?"

"Your question does not have an exact answer," Peggy replied.

"How so?"

"My first husband and I did divorce, but he is now deceased."

We did not talk at length but sufficiently to determine a dinner date was in order. Peggy gave me directions to her condominium for us to make the next Wednesday's pasta buffet at the Inn Of The Hills. While her picture on the internet was a bit dated, she was in fact as attractive in person as the image. Upon entry into her living room, I noted five large framed pastels of handsome young people. Peggy said, "They are my grandchildren. The boy's name is Clayton and he is my oldest." She then—in order of age—gave the names (Caitlin, Kristin, Savannah, and Madison) of the four girls and a brief description of each in a proud grandmotherly tone. "The portraits were done by Norman Schreiner. You may have seen his work."

"No, don't think I have. He is certainly very good."

"He did not get Kristin's head-shape correct. See how it is a little too pointed on top."

Right before we were about to exit her condo, Peggy stopped and said, "I want to make something very clear. I have had sex with only one man, and I was married to him." I thought, but did not say: *No problem; in less than two weeks a doctor in Houston will take care of that issue."* It was a short drive from Peggy's place to the restaurant. Peggy brought up religion, and I attempted to change the subject by giving my standard response. "That is a personal and private matter which I am not comfortable discussing." Normally that had been sufficient to stop further inquiry but not that night and not with Peggy. She persisted. Over dinner I described my loss-of-faith journey.

***

My surgery went well and the pathology report indicated the margins were clear. Now, ten years later, my PSA reading is still undetectable. It looks as if the doctors were correct. Kristi was there for my surgery, and she spent the night at the hospital. Sometime during the middle of that night, I awoke. Although still with residual of the anesthetic, I had a poignant, lucid thought: *I was alone. Kristi was asleep in the room, and I knew she loved me; but Stephen, Cale, and Addie were her number one priority—as they should be. Ola and Richard had welcomed me to recover in their home. They and my other family members care for me deeply. But the cold, hard truth remained: I was alone not just physically in a big empty house, but I was also spiritually alone.*

***

Existing while out-of-step with people I care about makes me uncomfortable. I do not feel uneasy because of a fear of being wrong. Being a majority of one is required at times for me to be true to myself. Within the basic nature of humans there is a longing for a greater guiding force. I thought the issue had been settled for me back in a summer while living in Naperville. Late in the year of 2004, at age sixty-six, I was not so sure.

The last (and most advanced) course in my minor undergraduate discipline was *Introduction to Modern Physics*. The professor closed his last lecture with the following statement: "I have a confession. Some of what we covered this semester is incorrect. My guess is more than one-third. Unfortunately, I don't know which one-third. That is both the beauty and bane of science. Foolish is the physicist who thinks humans can discern precisely and completely the elements in our space-time continuum. Science is not the pursuit of *facts* which can never be challenged. Quite the contrary, it demands a never-ending quest to try and explain the most insignificant unknown or inconsistency within current thinking." I believed my professor's words—and still do. It is ironic that I let go of the Divine and clung tightly to my faith of human-created science. But circumstances had changed my mind. I began to seek.

Dr. Michael Massar was the senior pastor of the First Baptist Church in Tyler, Texas. His counsel was, "Robert, if you are waiting for a *road to Damascus* type of communication from God, you are apt to be disappointed. You should be attuned to small items in daily living. Think of them as *nuggets* God has placed in your path, and they require attention or you will miss them." This advice would prove to be useful. I also sought input from Dr. John Petty the senior pastor at Trinity Baptist in Kerrville. John ended our discussion with, "Read one of the Gospels, and ask yourself the question 'Is Jesus who he said he is?' You need to have a *mustard seed* of faith when answering." I decided to do as John suggested. The Gospel According to Saint John was the selection.

I was not sure if there was a Bible in my empty house, until I remembered Daddy's ordination Bible. It was purchased by his Grandfather Godfrey. Grandfather Godfrey had anticipated that Daddy would be a preacher and planned to give the Bible to Daddy when ordained. He, my great-grandfather, did not live to give the Bible directly to my father. Thus, the post-mortem nature of the gift had an increased sentimental value. Some years after Daddy's death, Mother passed the Bible to me. It was a surprise since Darold was a preacher, so I had expected it would pass to him. After Mother's death, I told Shirley, "I am going to give the ordination Bible to Darold."

"Are you sure?"

"Why not? He is the minister."

"Your mother gave it to you. I think you should honor her desires."

I found the box with the Bible stored in the middle bedroom closet. The Bible had to be handled with care as it was worn from use. I opened it to the book of John and noticed Daddy had marked random verses. Without thinking I started reading the ones Daddy thought special. Twenty-seven verses were highlighted. There were two in the first chapter—verses twelve and twenty. Of course, verse sixteen of chapter three was included. Only once had Daddy selected two which were consecutive—verses twenty-five and twenty-six from chapter eleven. *Context* is to scripture as *location* is to real estate. But for me that night, Daddy's arbitrary medley was the precise perspective needed. My first read through ended with tears. During the second reading, I lingered on the last of the two consecutive verses—*And whosoever liveth and believeth in me shall never die.*

Believest thou this? I, like Martha, answered with, *"Yes, Lord: I believe."* That was easy since all it took was a little faith. But like an alcoholic trying to stay sober, attempting to understand the mystery of God is an ongoing pursuit.

Norman Schreiner portrait of Cale

Norman Schreiner portrait of Addie

Chapter 21

Moldova

There were only two or three hours after the dogs stopped barking before the roosters began to crow. Thus, Peggy's and my first night of sleep was short in the *honeymoon room* of the mission team-house in Chisinau, Moldova. We each awoke in the lower bunk of stacked beds. The top bunk-bed above me was covered with materials needed for a week's work for fifteen active ten-to-twelve-year old boys. Peggy's upper bunk-bed was also covered, but her supplies were for the older orphan boys. Our wedding date of August 1, 2006, had been less than two weeks prior. The ten days had been hectic. The death of Peggy's last sibling necessitated our departing directly from our wedding which was held in the chapel of the First Baptist Church in Comfort, Texas. Peggy's older sister's service was in Hastings, Oklahoma. The following day we arrived slightly before the funeral commenced. After a quick trip back to Kerrville, we finished getting ready for the mission trip to Moldova.

Moldova had been part of the Soviet Union and gained its independence after the fall of the Berlin Wall. The Transnistria area on Moldova's border with Ukraine was still in dispute and occupied by Russian military troops. The Moldovans were in the process of developing the elements of a market-based democracy. One legacy of their recent communist past was a large number of children who were wards of the state. Some were true orphans with no living parent. There were also those whose parents were too poor to provide the basic necessities for themselves, much less their off-spring. Last were the abandoned children. For the school year these dependents were housed and attended classes in state boarding schools. These schools had responsibility for their students until completion of grade-nine. Then the youth were on their own and became very vulnerable—possible human trafficking for the girls and crime for the boys. During the summer break the boarding schools closed, and the government placed as many as possible with whomever they could—mostly grandparents, aunts, uncles, and older siblings. The ones with no one to receive them were sent to summer camps. The camps' facilities had been used by the communist youth (Komsomol) during the soviet era. By the turn of the century, most of these camps were in disrepair. A few teachers shepherded the children during summer camp. But there were no planned activities, and the government welcomed outsiders to bring programs for the children. Trinity Baptist Church first sent a mission team to Moldova in the summer of 2005. They worked at a camp in a rural setting which was a forty-five minute rough van ride from the Chisinau team-house. Peggy was a member of that group. Our plans in 2006 were for me to fly with the team to Frankfurt, Germany. I would then take a train to Switzerland and visit friends while Peggy and the other team members were in Moldova. James Ellis, who had gone in 2005, had a last-minute medical emergency and had to cancel for 2006. Linda Worden, the team leader, asked if I would change plans and fill-in for James. I agreed to do so.

The team house could accommodate about twenty people, and our team was only fifteen. Thus, Peggy and I had a room to ourselves. The house had three levels. Female team members used the lower level. Our room was on the main floor with the kitchen, utility room, and dining area. Men slept in the top flats. There was also an apartment in the third level for the Moldovan mission director and her husband. Their apartment was air conditioned as were the kitchen and dining room. All other spaces used floor fans to circulate the humid, warm night air. Most of the other team members' rooms were like ours, with beds for four. But we had our own bathroom. In the women's basement one of the rooms had a bath, and the other rooms shared a common bath which had three showers. On the men's floor there was just one shower with little pressure and no hot water if the women got to their showers first.

The team's day began with a good breakfast prepared by Lydia, the cook and cleaning lady. After a brief devotional from one of the team members, we left to be at the camp near ten in the morning. A large group of the children were there to greet us and help carry items to the gazebo. All the children were welcomed to the gazebo for singing, skits, slide-shows, and videos. Attendance for our activities was strictly voluntary. But they loved to sing, so except for a few of the oldest boys, almost all the campers were in the gazebo as our corps of young interpreters set up the sound system, prepared the song sheets, connected the laptop with the projector, and placed the screen. This was done with the *assistance* of dozens of little *helping* hands. The younger children jockeyed for the laps of team members. If all laps were taken, any spot with physical contact was their fallback strategy. There was lots of pushing, shouting, and shoving by the middle-aged children for the most coveted locations for viewing. It was a scene of marginally controlled chaos. I confess it perturbed me during that first year. But each time I returned (I made eight mission trips), my attitude improved. I got to know many of the children, and they knew me. It became an uplifting and rewarding experience.

There was one interchange during the first trip which was sobering. It happened near the end of the week during the afternoon's free-time. I was under a shade tree next to the soccer field with an interpreter and four or five of the boys from my morning Bible study group. I was showing them pictures. One was of my house. An older boy joined us and snatched the photo from the hands of one of my boys, saying (via the interpreter) "If I lived near you, I would rob you."

I responded with a question, "Why would you do that?"

He then said in a softer tone, "I was kidding."

"May I ask you a serious question?" my question created a puzzled look on his face but no reply. So I continued, "What do you hope to be doing in ten years?"

His tone changed back to defiance, "Why do you want to know?"

"I don't know much about Moldova and was wondering if you believe stealing is your only option to survive when you finish boarding school."

"Why do you care?"

"I am here. Does that count?"

I could tell he was not convinced. Perhaps the adult world had failed him too often. *What can an old man from Texas do—even if he does care?* This was a reasonable thought he might have had. I really wanted to know his answer. So I persisted, "Sergiu, I understand your doubts of my motives, but I would appreciate knowing your hopes for the future."

In a reserved manner he said, "If I am alive...." He gave a complete answer that included shoe repair or van driver, but his first four words gave me pause—*if I am alive....* It is sad that any thirteen-year-old boy begins a statement about his possible future with "*if I am alive....*"

***

Peggy and I headed south from Frankfurt on the autobahn toward the Bavarian Alps. A week of working with the children during the day and long nights of preparation had left us exhausted. A few mornings of sleeping late with lazy afternoons of sight-seeing were our plans before returning to Kerrville. It was late afternoon when we came off the autobahn and were funneled to a two-lane highway labeled *OAL 1*. We did not have an exact destination in mind and spotted a small village off to the right. With a little effort, the only hotel in town was found. Hurriedly we checked in and unloaded all our stuff. There was just enough daylight to see the sunset over Neuschwanstein castle. Peggy grabbed a light jacket and her camera. I noted the name of the village did not contain many letters and focused on the scenic beauty with little attention given to landmarks. We dined in a quaint restaurant associated with a small hotel located on the side of a mountain with a panoramic view of the castle. The food was good, and the sunset scene spectacular as the fairy-tale structure changed from daylight charm to the illuminated splendor of darkness.

Within fifteen minutes after leaving the restaurant to return to our rented room which contained all we had except Peggy's camera and the clothes we had on, I knew we were lost. Our rented car did not have a GPS. All maps and travel materials were in a hotel, the name of which neither of us could remember. Heck, we didn't even know the name of the town. There were neither cars nor people on the dark rural road. Soon we came to a traffic circle with four outlets in addition to the one we were on. The good news was all indicated the name of the town to which each was headed, and only one name was short—*Seeg*. The bad news was that road was barricaded due to road repairs. I selected the road next to the one to Seeg, and Peggy wrote down the name of the town from which we had come.

Only a bar was open, and the bartender and two French tourists were of little help. We encountered a middle-aged couple in the streets. She was tight, and her husband was drunk. Not falling-down drunk, but close. Our situation helped me to stay attuned so I knew how to return to the restaurant. Going back there seemed the best option. When we got back, only two customers and the owner were there. The owner knew the name of our hotel in Seeg and gave us directions. Her directions were clear except for which street to take after circling a church in a town between us and Seeg. There was absolutely no living soul in sight as we sat beside that church debating which route to take. Suddenly a car driven by a young man pulled up beside us, and in perfect English, he said, "Do you need help?"

"Yes, we are trying to get to Seeg."

"Follow me."

I pulled in behind him as he drove off. Soon after we left the town limits a second auto came close behind us but did not pass. These were the only two moving vehicles we had seen since leaving the restaurant the first time. I was concerned and slowed to a very low speed. The car behind soon passed both us and our benevolent stranger. We thanked the young man as he turned around at the edge of Seeg. We entered our hotel five minutes before the eleven o'clock closing.

Lesson Time (left) Play Time (right)

Chapter 22

Bittersweet

In September of 2011, I wrote the following note.

Sometimes feelings, emotions, and thoughts can come into clearer focus if put on paper. That is my objective.

It seems Peggy and I both have a need (or want) that is an imperative to avoid a feeling of discontentment. Our individual need/want seems to be an integral part of who we are. Peggy's need/want is not mine, and vice versa. In addition to being different, they are mutually exclusive. A marriage has an impossible obstacle to overcome if both husband and wife have different imperative needs/wants, and if the meeting of one's automatically excludes the fulfillment of the other's.

My memory and understanding of the marriage counselor's analysis of our basic problem is one of these needs dilemmas. He also expressed his belief that the Moldova incident and its aftermath were outward manifestations of this more basic problem. He indicated Peggy has a strong need for assurance from me that she is number one. My need is for who I am to be enough to satisfy.

I suspect a third party might wonder "What is the problem?- Robert, just make sure Peggy knows she is the most important, and life will be great!" But, life is not so straightforward, because actions are subject to different interpretations, and the Moldova incident and its aftermath is a prime example. The short period of time in the team room in August, 2010 exposed how different views of the same event can create a major fault line in a relationship.

*My understanding of our different opinions is as follows: Peggy believes I intentionally put another woman number one. Peggy's reaction then and in the months since indicates she believes I was guilty of some type of "emotional infidelity," and she strongly believes most any rational wife would agree with her. This is not how I view it. I was being who I am in helping another team member. I was wrong in not being attentive to Peggy's need for help, and I apologized for that. But, there were **absolutely no** inappropriate "male-female" actions or thoughts by me that night or any other time while working with my co-teacher. If Peggy's view is correct, then I committed a major act of betrayal, and regaining her trust would justify a major effort by me. But, what if Peggy has misinterpreted my actions? Then her prolonged verbal abuse to get me to acknowledge the severity of my transgression and do things to heal the hurt has been very corrosive to our relationship. In fact, I now have little confidence in Peggy's judgment of me and my future actions. Only God completely knows my heart and mind, and I stand ready to answer for all my actions and thoughts that night and the year since. I* *have confessed to God, Peggy, three counselors, my co-teacher and her spouse, and John & Linda Worden concerning the fact that I was so involved in a task that I did not hear and thus did not respond to Peggy's request for help in a timely manner. I have not, and will not admit to making another woman more important to me than Peggy; because I have not. Perhaps if I am lying to myself about this, the Holy Spirit will give me a revelation. But I have requested that revelation, and it has not come.*

I naively thought we could get past this issue by just not talking about it. I now realize that is not true. Peggy needs me to accept her hurt and my perceived betrayal and reestablish her trust. I need Peggy to believe in the purity of my heart and take actions to regain my confidence. Neither is apt to happen, and being mutually exclusive, a compromise is not possible.

It surprises me how often Peggy's and my views have not been aligned concerning the same event. For the most part, our different thought processes are not a problem because so much of life is not that critical. But a big one, such as the Moldova incident, can bring hurt and pain almost beyond belief.

Our interim pastor recently said one's home should be a place of encouragement. Over a year ago my brief, inadvertent act created an atmosphere in which not only did Peggy not feel encouragement, but there was an unacceptable level of discouragement for her. I have done my best to right this wrong, but my efforts have not been successful. There have been some good and fun times during the last year, but for me, the times of emotional insecurity have greatly overshadowed these positive times. I know it has been a very difficult and unhealthy time for Peggy also.

If my observations included in this document are valid, then I see no hope for our continued marriage. I make that statement after much prayer and reflection. The probability of our having such different interpretations of similar incidents in the future is just too high for my comfort level.

I filed for divorce soon after writing this account. The Moldova incident referred to in the account occurred on Wednesday night of the Trinity Baptist Church's mission trip in August 2010. I was engrossed in helping my co-teacher print pictures of our boys taken with her cell phone. We were working at the dining table in the team-house. The desktop computer used by team members was in the same room. At times it was difficult to connect to the internet. I had better luck and helped Peggy and others get online after they failed. Peggy stated that she came into the room and requested my help, but I did not respond. I believe that Peggy did ask for my assistance and certainly received no immediate response from me. Peggy's reaction, or should I say *overreaction,* resulted in nearly a year of her having sporadic outbursts of anger and rage. One of the many things she said to me later that night was, "I can make your life a living hell." I did not agree with much of what she said that night, but that statement proved to be absolutely true.

When Peggy came into the room and spoke to me that fateful night, my total focus was on trying to get pictures printed. That was the reason she did not get my immediate attention. It was not—I repeat—was not because I wanted to *treat her like dirt* or was *too busy trying to impress my co-teacher*. I did not *intentionally humiliate my wife while laughing and having a fun time with a younger woman*. If Peggy had just come over and touched my arm as suggested by the first marriage counselor, I would have stopped what I was doing and helped her. Incidentally, when the counselor suggested that would have been a more appropriate action, Peggy shouted at him, and he proposed the need for sessions with her only. When she came home early from their second private meeting, I asked why. Peggy indicated they had some type of disagreement, she walked out and she was not going to see him again.

Peggy did apologize for her eruptions of fury. However, her regret came with a major caveat—she was sorry for the shouting and angry tone, but she stood firm concerning the truth of the content. It hurts when the one you loved thinks you are *a liar*.

***

My lawyer and I were in the office of Judge Spencer Brown for no more than ten minutes, and Spencer talked of golf as much as the document in front of him.

"Robert, is all the information in this decree correct?" he asked.

"To the best of my knowledge, it is."

"Good enough for me," Judge Brown said to my lawyer and signed the Final Decree of Divorce. The date was March 26, 2012, more than a year and a half after the Moldova incident. I removed the gold band from the third finger of my left hand upon exiting Judge Brown's chambers. My emotions were neither relief nor sadness, only a numb pale of unavoidable failure.

Chapter 23

Transition

I moved from the rented apartment back into my house. It looked a bit snaggletoothed but felt oh so comfortable—like a well-worn pair of blue jeans. I felt no trace of emptiness. Peggy had removed her furniture from the big room, guest bedroom, breakfast nook, and office. I relocated my office setup from the third bedroom back to its original location. There were four areas which needed furnishings. All but the breakfast area could wait. I purchased a very used table with two chairs from the man next to me at the apartment complex. He had loaned them to me when he learned I was eating off a card table.

I sorted and culled my junk. This should have been done after Shirley's death. Back then I was able with Kristi's help to donate Shirley's clothes to charity and had good intentions to clean out the entire house. But somehow it never happened. Now I culled with vigor. It took over two months, and there was a good feeling of accomplishment when completed. Next, the big room became my main project as I assumed the role of interior decorator. There were only three items in the twenty-by thirty-foot room—a behind-the-sofa metal table with a glass top, a stained-glass hanging, and my cow bell from Switzerland. The bare table went back into the entry nook, and I left the stained glass and cow bell untouched. My first action was a trip to a Scandinavian furnishings store in San Antonio. A sales woman greeted me, "May I help you?"

"I am looking for furniture for the big room in my house. The house does not have a formal living area."

"What pieces will you want?"

"I guess a sofa, love seat, and side chair."

"Do you have anything particular in mind?"

"No."

"Let me show you a few possibilities."

On our way to the living room section we passed by a dining set which was similar to mine. I stopped to check the price. It was about $1,500 for the table. This was not much more than the $1,304 we paid to The Happy Viking of New Jersey, Importer of fine Scandinavian furnishings. I commented, "About the same amount as I paid."

"When did you buy yours?"

"1987."

"Do you know the manufacturer?"

"I know it was made in Denmark and think the company's name was *Glostrup*."

"Sir, hang on to your table. It is solid teak. The one you just saw is veneer. We do not stock solid teak tables like yours."

"Why not?"

"I am not sure if they are still produced. But even if available, the price would be prohibitive for most people."

The exchange with the sales person gave me inspiration for a design concept. My big room and dining area are not separated by a wall. They flow together with a six foot wide opening. Thus, the main pieces in the big room would be exposed teak wood style matching the look of the dining room. Finding sofas and love seats with exposed hard wood proved to be difficult and especially so for teak. Pictures in a catalog were the best I could do. Therefore, I ordered items never tested for comfort. The style of teak furniture once constructed in

Denmark is now made in Thailand. It was more than a year before the three-cushion sofa, two-cushion love seat, and matching side chair arrived in Kerrville. During that year of waiting, I selected photographs taken by Addie—most of vivid colored flowers, highlighted by digitally composed backgrounds. The backgrounds were either all black or all white. A collage of these pictures became the focal point in the big room.

***

Cale and Addie were growing up. In the school year 2010-2011 Cale was a senior and Addie a sophomore at Pearsall High School. Maybe it was that year or perhaps a year or two before that a tradition began. Both my grandchildren were active in athletics. Cale played football, basketball, and baseball. In basketball his passing skills were good. When Cale was in Little Dribblers his coach had him do the in-bounds passing. In high school his three-point shooting was better than average. I remember a game when he made four, and he did not shoot very often. Addie played some basketball but not the last years of high school. She did well in volleyball. However, Addie was first and foremost a runner (I'll take some credit). It started early. In daycare she blacked both eyes hitting a brick wall while racing a male classmate. At elementary track meets there was an event when the kids were timed as they ran around the baseball diamond. The coach at home base normally allowed a runner to leave as the child in front rounded first base. She held Addie until the boy ahead was at second, and still he reached home only two or three strides ahead of Addie. She was a regional qualifier in both the 1600 and 3200 meters during her freshman year.

Like a proud grandfather I began talking about my grandchildren and forgot about the tradition mentioned earlier. I baked cookies for Cale and Addie's teams. Not just any *ole cookies* but *the best chocolate chip goodies this side of the Rio Grande.* At least that was what the kids said. Perhaps they understood stroking my ego kept the sweets coming. I must 'fess up. I used a mix which required adding only a stick of butter and an egg. Perchance, could it have been the uncalled for half-cup of sixty percent cocoa bits that did the trick? For whatever reason, my cookies are my legacy with Cale and Addie's teammates. Not a bad way to be remembered.

In the spring of 2011, I sat in the top row of Pearsall's football stadium and listened as my grandson Cale gave the valedictory address at his class's commencement exercises. Two years later it was Addie's night to be honored as the highest rank in her graduating class.

***

Finding a new church home was also on my to-do list. Many friends from Trinity Baptist Church reached out to me. Their kindness and encouragement were very helpful and appreciated. However, Peggy and I had agreed it best if we did not attend the same church. Peggy was a long-time member of Trinity. So I would find a different congregation in which to worship and serve. It was not easy to leave Trinity—one more downer resulting from our divorce. I had attended the men's Wednesday morning Bible study at the Methodist church. Therefore, I attended Sunday services there first. While the worship was meaningful, it was not the best fit for me. I sought input from a friend. He asked me a few questions, and after my responses he then said, "Have you visited a Presbyterian church?"

"No. I haven't even considered it."

"Based on what you just told me, and what I know about you. I think you should."

The next Sunday morning I stood at the back of the sanctuary of the First Presbyterian Church looking for the best place to sit. The selection process is a delicate mix of art and science. Visiting different churches the last few weeks had honed my instincts and skills. First, just because a place is vacant does not mean it is available. It may *belong* to a member in good standing who has sat there for twenty years. Only the most astute visitor discerns the *empty-but-reserved* locations on the first visit. Most learn of them by trial and error. A place in the front row will always be open. But I won't use it because of why it is untaken. In Kerrville, forget about pews two to four—maybe because of the number of members with hearing or sight issues. The back two or three rows are taken quickly as are the seats adjacent to any aisle. I did not hesitate long that Sunday morning before selecting a spot near the middle of the fourth row from the rear. Now that seat *belongs* to me. I did make one slight error. Being a recovering Baptist, I did not understand the pulpit-lectern system, and my seat is not on the sermon delivery side.

After a couple of Sundays, Presbyterianism seemed suitable. I made an appointment with Bill and Betty Byrd. Their marriage was a second for both. Their respective spouses had died. Betty and her first husband were members of First Presbyterian where she is an Elder. Bill and his first wife were active in Trinity Baptist. Bill was my Sunday school teacher. They were splitting attendance. Bill had recently switched so they would be members of the same congregation. I was encouraged after our discussion which covered a wide range of issues. They recommended I meet with Associate Pastor Rob Lohmeyer. After meeting with Rob, I became a member of First Presbyterian Church in late May of 2012.

***

Fred Kapelle answered when I called the number in the church newsletter. I asked, "Is this the Kapelle residence?"

"Yes."

"Are you Fred?"

"Yes, I am."

"Fred, I am Robert Baldwin and am calling in reference to the notice in the most recent Windmill concerning training for Stephen Ministry."

"Are you familiar with the ministry?" Fred asked.

"All I know is what I have read from the small blue cards in the holders on the backs of the pews."

Fred then explained, "To become a Stephen Minister is a little different than most other church service opportunities in that you must first complete an application. The forms are in the church office. After your application has been reviewed there will be an interview by two or three Stephen Ministers who have been trained as leaders. If accepted, you must complete fifty hours of formal training and agree to at least two years of service. We are trying to get a class started soon."

The church certified five other training-class members and me as Stephen Ministers on February 17, 2013.

***

I have a theory. Actually I have many, but this one seems relevant. If a mentally and physically healthy person has a normal life cycle and dies of natural causes, he starts life focused on himself—food and diaper changes. With age his horizon expands to include others—first it is family and then friends. Years of increasing diversity are the standard until at some point the circle of interests starts to contract. It will continue to decrease until the person is in a fetal position on his death bed. Then it becomes difficult to be attuned to a world with a population greater than one. Believing this to be true, I have attempted to keep myself in the growth mode as long as possible. But deterioration of mind and body has imposed unwanted reductions of attentiveness. Like it or not, my life is shrinking. The best I can do is to take actions to slow the process—golf and walking help physically and emotionally. Writing this book is my current project for my mind. Spiritual stenosis is too often an affliction of the non-sovereign elderly. Independence and selfishness can easily become inversely proportional with aging. But it is not inevitable. It is enriching to be near a person at the end stages of his life who maintains a concern for others. I hope I have and will keep that type of personality.

Kristi, Stephen, Cale, Addie

Big Room with new furniture & Addie's collage

Chapter 24

Twilight Love

The Boyds stayed in contact with Shirley and me after our undergraduate days, though there were periods of silence due to distance and demands of daily life—children and careers as young adults, and health issues as we aged. While we were in Walsenburg, Darrell and Janie were in Shallowater. Darrell was teaching mathematics at the same school where Janie had graduated as valedictorian of the class of 1956. Janie was expecting their first child when Darrell and I walked across that temporary stage at Texas Tech on May 29, 1961. Gregory Edwin Boyd was born almost exactly one month later on June 30, 1961. Darrell and Janie visited during our summer of leisure in the mountains of Colorado; this became routine as Darrell and Janie visited Shirley and me everywhere we lived—including Puerto Rico and Switzerland. I joke but it is true that even my own mother did not come to see me in New Jersey, but the Boyds did. Janie gave birth to a daughter, Lori Denise, on September 13, 1963, seven months after Kristi arrived. Darrell was still teaching in Shallowater at the time. Two years later he decided to make a change and obtained a position in the Tahoka school district. When I learned Darrell had resigned from Shallowater, I considered the possibility of his coming to Amarillo. It was an easy sell, equivalent pay without a school bus route. I had hoped he would be assigned to Tascosa, but instead Darrell became a faculty member at Amarillo High School. He taught there for the next twenty-seven years. Janie's first years out of high school mirrored Shirley's. Both attended Tech for one semester and then worked to put their husbands through college. Janie took a different path once in Amarillo. She went back to school—first to

Amarillo College and then West Texas State—and earned a Bachelor of Arts degree in 1969 and a Master of Education in 1981. Janie earned the Master's while teaching junior high English and Spanish. The last years of her professional career were as the librarian at Crockett Middle School. Janie retired in 1996 after twenty-six plus years.

***

In the summer of 1997 Darrell, Lynn Jones, and I played a round of golf at Hunsley Hills in Canyon. Shirley had told me Janie had some concerns about Darrell's memory, but I had detected nothing other than normal aging. During the round of golf, I changed my mind. First, Darrell asked me to keep score. He had always done the score keeping. On a par four hole early in the round: Darrell was on the green in regulation, I was short in the frog-hair, and Lynn's ball was hidden in the tall grass under a tree beside the green. The three of us found Lynn's ball after a short search. Lynn and I had bogies, and Darrell two-putted for his par. Walking to the next tee I asked Darrell his score. He said, "Five."

"Are you sure? I thought you shot par."

"Was that ball under the tree mine or Lynn's?"

"It was Lynn's."

"Then I did have a four."

I immediately realized that Darrell for sure had short-term memory issues, but it had not affected his honesty.

***

I remember well the day in 1998 when Darrell and Janie came to see us. It was an unexpected visit. After catching up on family news, Janie turned to Darrell and asked, "Don't you have something to tell Robert and Shirley?" Seated on the couch in the big room of our Kerrville home, Darrell gave us the sad news, "I have this malady." Shirley and I did not respond, waiting to hear more. Darrell turned to Janie and said, "What is it called, Janie? I can't remember."

"Alzheimers."

The word hung in the air like a dark cloud for a few silent seconds until I asked, "How do you know?" Darrell had always been quiet by nature, but normally he would have responded. Now, he looked at Janie, as if a child deferring to an adult.

Janie replied, "I have had suspicions for some time. Recently the doctor confirmed that my observations were consistent with his diagnosis. The doctor prescribed Aricept which he thinks has a possibility to plateau, or at least slow the disease."

Never had I talked to an Alzheimers patient. I directed my questions to Darrell, "Do you understand what it means?"

"I sure do," was his response.

"Are you scared?"

"I am terrified." He replied with a look in his eyes which answered my question even if he had not opened his mouth.

During the time between their visit in 1998 and Shirley's death, we saw little of each other. Per a telephone request from me, Janie wrote one of the memorials read at Shirley's service. Darrell's condition prevented their attendance. A few weeks after the spreading of Shirley's ashes, I called Janie to inquire about Darrell.

"He is not doing well."

"Does he still play golf?"

"No, but he was able to get to and from the golf course longer than to and from other locations. Ira Guthrie picked him up after the doctor recommended Darrell stop driving."

"I did not know Darrell could not drive. How is he handling it?"

"Surprisingly well. When the doctor gave Darrell the news, he took the keys from his pocket and without complaint gave them to me."

After additional exchanges about family and common friends I said, "I would like to come and see Darrell if you think it wise."

"I think he will remember you and enjoy your visit, but within five minutes after you leave, he will not even remember you were here.

During my visit, Darrell and I reminisced about our college days while seated in the living room. His memory of our study times was better than mine. However, it was heartbreaking that his once-nimble mind could not recall anything that happened five minutes before. As I headed south from Amarillo toward Kerrville, I felt the goodbyes exchanged with my dear friend would be our last. There were tears, but not until I was alone on the road. Of course, the person whom I had just left was a shell of Darrell's once reserved but also mischievous personality. My infrequent visits spared me the agony of experiencing Darrell's gradual decline as his cruel *malady* maliciously and slowly dissolved his true personhood. It did give me empathy for Janie and the other loved ones who walked that path with Darrell. Darrell died on Sunday October 16, 2005, ten days before his sixty-ninth birthday. I served as a pallbearer at his funeral.

During my last visit with Darrell.

Janie and I checked on each other from time to time until my relationship with Peggy became serious. Janie's and my friendship was platonic. However, I stepped back from further contact because of my love for Peggy. My next contact with Janie was after I had filed for divorce and was living in an apartment separate from Peggy. It was in the late fall of 2011. Our first telephone conversations were just between friends catching up on the previous five years. I talked often about the failure of my marriage, but news from Kristi, Stephen, Cale, and Addie was also a prime topic. Janie updated me on Greg and Lori and their activities. There was an unwanted surprise—Janie has retinitis pigmentosa. I was not familiar with the disease, so Janie educated me. In her case, it had restricted her field of vision, and the damage was permanent and progressive. She could no longer drive. Our conversations increased over time and became longer in duration. By January of 2012 Janie had become my *telephone psychiatrist.*

Isaiah Richard Lawrence, Janie's great-grandson, was to be baptized in the Hillsboro United Methodist Church on April 22, 2012. Hillsboro is a suburb of Portland, Oregon. How might Janie be able to attend? Flying alone was not viable. Voncille Fountain, a dear friend, had accompanied Janie two years earlier for the baptism of Isaiah's older brother Darrell. Schedule conflicts prevented Voncille from going. I had time and had made a commitment to myself to be more helpful toward friends. Don McClintock was a case in point. He had major issues with Parkinsons for which I was able to give much support. My calendar was open for me to escort Janie, and I looked forward to a trip with a longtime friend and meeting some members of her family. Besides I had never visited Portland. My job was to be a *better set of eyes*. I enjoyed Janie's family and had time to do some exploring on my own.

Disaster almost struck the morning we left early in the darkness for our return flight. The Lawrence's house sits on a hillside with outside steps. Low light and stair steps are very difficult for Janie. Descending in front of me, she missed a step. The next few seconds seemed to be in slow motion. Janie was a few steps above a concrete landing, and it seemed certain she would hit the bottom with damaging force. Instead of falling head-first downward Janie fell to the right toward the side of the house and reflexively pushed off the house. She fell to the left, avoided the unforgiving surface, and landed hard on a grassy knoll. Janie's granddaughter, Barbara, flew past me to the rescue. Barbara helped Janie up, and she was fine. Janie should have fired her *seeing-eye-dog* that morning, but I'm happy that she didn't.

***

I awoke on the first day of 2013 with no plans. There might have been a football bowl game I wanted to watch later in the day. But after breakfast, I was free. "This is the perfect time to begin writing my book," I thought aloud. So I began. After an hour or two and many false starts, the words *How many more tomorrows do I have?* became the top line of an otherwise blank page. How was I going to get from this opening question to the end of Part One? The draft of chapter one took about two weeks.

***

Gene Streun passed away in early February of 2013. Cynthia asked me to serve as an honorary pallbearer for his service in Hereford. Being near Amarillo meant I could reconnect with landmarks to include in the Amarillo chapter of my book. Janie and I regularly had long telephone conversations, so she was the first to hear what I had written. I also e-mailed Janie a copy of each chapter, and she in turn corrected my spelling and grammar. Janie agreed to ride with me as I tried to rekindle the sights and sounds of my days as a young high school teacher in Amarillo. I don't remember exactly where or what it was, but something stirred my emotions to tears—this was not unusual, since I choke-up easily. Janie said nothing at the time but simply reached over and lightly touched my shoulder. Was it empathy, or was it something more? It is one thing to understand another's pain, but quite another to feel that pain. Janie's glance and touch caused surprising feelings, and I followed up on them that evening. Seated on Janie's love seat, we were having a pleasant conversation when I experienced a sudden rush of passion. Janie's presence in the future would be different than the past in ways unknown to me during that blissful moment. I tentatively leaned toward her and we kissed, and Janie playfully said, "We had better be careful or we might destroy a good friendship." I disregarded the warning and kissed her long and passionately. Marriage was not really in our future since Janie was very content living in Amarillo. She had family, friends, and church. There was a group of her friends which was her *taxi team*. Amarillo's major shopping mall was only a block away. Her life was settled and good, as was mine.

I fired up my computer to start writing on February 16, 2013, and found an e-mail from Janie which read in part:

> *I'm not proposing, but let's revisit the subject of marriage. I know you have good reason to avoid it. As for me, my immediate thought was "No, I don't want to marry again.". . . sometime, would you list the pros and cons you have about marriage? Then I'll do the same....*

I sent my list quickly, and just minutes after it was gone, my phone rang.

"Nine cons and only three pros?" Janie quizzed

"It's not the number but the importance of each, and the pros win that race by a mile," I replied. We talked of our love and faith in each other, and of the future pleasures and difficulties we would share together.

***

"What inscription will you want on the wedding band?" The sales woman asked.

Janie and I had selected a gold band to go with her sapphire and diamond engagement ring. Actually we chose two thin ones—one for each side of the engagement ring. I bought one for our wedding—and the second would wait until our first anniversary. The clerk's question was regarding the first ring.

"Robert, you are buying the ring for me. You decide."

I had an inspiration, "How about *Twilight Love Is a Blessing*." Janie liked it, and it became the theme of our wedding and marriage. We became husband and wife on June 29, 2013, two days after Janie's seventy-fifth birthday. Darold led the ceremony, and his wife Lynn was our organist. All others in our wedding party were also family members. There were about 100 guests including James and Marjorie Ellis, and Oscar and Joan Brantley who drove from Kerrville to Amarillo. Janie sold her house in Amarillo and moved to Kerrville.

In a scene near the end of the movie, *Shawshank Redemption*, the main character says to his friend, "I guess it comes down to a simple choice really, get busy living or get busy dying."

Janie and I are busy living.

Janie and me June 29, 2013

Epilogue

At the end of Chapter 1, I indicated my desires concerning my ashes after death. Herein I amend my request as follows: If I die before Janie, a small portion of my ashes shall be retained to be interred with her. However, if Janie dies before me, I would like a small amount of my ashes spread on her grave in the cemetery at Amarillo.

Back Row L-R: Tyson Garner, David Garner, Darrell Lawrence, Greg Boyd, Matt Boyd, Isaiah Lawrence, Ben Lawrence, Heath Moore. Middle Row L-R: Lori Boyd Garner, Missy Boyd, Barbara Boyd Lawrence, Jamie Garner Moore. Front Row: Janie & me

Addie, Janie, Stephen, me, Cale, Kristi